Language Teaching:
A Scheme for Teacher Education

Editors: C N Candlin and H G Widdowson

Classroom Interaction

Ann Malamah-Thomas

Oxford University Press
1987

Oxford University Press
Walton Street, Oxford OX2 6DP

Oxford New York Toronto
Delhi Bombay Calcutta Madras Karachi
Petaling Jaya Singapore Hong Kong Tokyo
Nairobi Dar es Salaam Cape Town
Melbourne Auckland

and associated companies in
Beirut Berlin Ibadan Nicosia

OXFORD is a trade mark of Oxford University Press

ISBN 0 19 437131 X

© Oxford University Press 1987

Typeset in Sabon by Wyvern Typesetting Ltd, Bristol
Printed and bound in Great Britain by
R. J. Acford, Chichester, West Sussex.

Acknowledgements

The publisher would like to thank the following for their permission to
reproduce material that falls within their copyright:

Addison-Wesley for extracts from *Analysing Teaching Behavior* (1970) by
N. A. Flanders.

R. G. Bowers for an extract from his PhD thesis 'Verbal Behaviour in the
Language Teaching Classroom' (University of Reading, 1980).

The British Council for extracts from *Communication Games* (1979) and
Teaching and Learning in Focus (1985).

Harper and Row for an exercise from *Caring and Sharing in the Foreign
Language Classroom* (Newbury House, 1978) by Gertrude Moskowitz.

Longman Group for an exercise from *The Elements of Direct and Indirect
Speech* (1965) by Donn Byrne.

Methuen for six figures from *Microteaching* (1975) by George Brown.

R. Mitchell and B. Parkinson for a table from their paper given at the 1979
BAAL conference: 'A Systematic Linguistic Analysis of the Strategies of Foreign
Language Teaching in the Secondary School'.

Pergamon Press for extracts from 'Approaches to observation in second-
language classes' by R. Ullmann and E. Geva (in *ELT Documents 119:
Language Issues and Education Policies*, ed. C. J. Brumfit, 1984).

Royal Society of Arts Examinations Board for an extract from the Check List
and Report on Practical Test for the Diploma for Overseas Teachers of English.

Contents

The author and series editors

Ann Malamah-Thomas is a graduate of the University of Edinburgh, where she read English Language and Literature. Since 1970 she has worked for the British Council as a teacher and teacher trainer, mainly in Turkey and Sierra Leone, but also in Peru and six Western European countries. In 1980 she won a prize awarded by the English Speaking Union for her work on reading in EFL. She has published a book on using the language laboratory, and several articles on aspects of classroom methodology. She is currently serving as the British Council Assistant Representative with responsibility for English language teaching in Bangladesh.

Christopher Candlin is Professor of Linguistics in the School of English and Linguistics at Macquarie University, Sydney, having previously been Professor of Applied Linguistics and Director of the Centre for Language in Social Life at the University of Lancaster. He also co-founded and directed the Institute for English Language Education at Lancaster, where he worked on issues in in-service education for teachers.

Henry Widdowson is Professor of English for Speakers of Other Languages at the University of London Institute of Education, having previously been Lecturer in Applied Linguistics at the University of Edinburgh. Before that, he worked on materials development and teacher education as a British Council English Language Officer in Sri Lanka and Bangladesh.

Through work with The British Council, The Council of Europe, and other agencies, both Editors have had extensive and varied experience of language teaching, teacher education, and curriculum development overseas, and both contribute to seminars, conferences, and professional journals.

Introduction

Classroom Interaction

Learning a language, like the learning of anything else, is essentially an individual achievement, an exploitation of the capacities of the mind to make sense of the environment. But typically this private process takes place in the public context of the classroom, the individual is one of a group, a member of the class, and the activities which are to set the process in train are determined by the teacher. The assumption is that this internal process of learning will come about as a consequence of the external interaction which takes place between the two kinds of participant: the teacher on the one hand, and the learners on the other. The classroom interaction serves an enabling function: its only purpose is to provide conditions for learning.

There is something of a paradox here. Although teaching is a subservient activity, accountable entirely to its effect on learning, the teacher typically assumes a dominant and directive role in classroom interaction, and it is learning which is made accountable to the teaching intent. Thus, traditionally, learning has been seen as the reflex of teaching, the action of the teacher as requiring a corresponding reaction on the part of the learner. Learners may be induced to co-operate by *overt* participation in the classroom interaction, either with the teacher or with other learners in groups, but there may be conflicts with the *covert* processes of individual learning itself. More recently there have been proposals to reduce this requirement of conformity and to allow learners to take a greater initiative. But this initiative can be effectively exercised only within some set of bearings which will provide it with direction and purpose. The question is: what kind of classroom interaction, what kinds of participation of teacher and learner, are most likely to provide conditions whereby the exercise of individual learner initiative can lead to effective learning?

Whatever pedagogic approach is taken, it is the interaction of the classroom, the assumption and assignment of different kinds of participant role, which mediates between teaching and learning. It is therefore of crucial importance that the factors which enter into this interaction should be subjected to careful and critical examination and their implications for pedagogic practice explored in the context of actual classrooms. It is the purpose of this book to stimulate such examination and exploration, so that teachers too can take the initiative in learning, through their own experience of teaching, the effective exercise of the craft of pedagogy.

This book, in common with others in the scheme, consists of three sections. The first leads the reader into different ways of *defining* the classroom encounter conceptually in terms of its interactive and communicative features; and operationally in relation to the analysis of different aspects of learner and teacher activity.

Section Two then relates the defining concepts introduced in Section One to ways of *describing* different aspects of classroom interaction. It provides the opportunity for readers to subject to critical scrutiny, informed by their own teaching experience, the schemes that have been devised for the systematic description of classroom behaviour, and various recent approaches to pedagogy which have particular implications for the learner's participation in classroom interaction.

In Section Three, the reader is then provided with the means for *exploring* by direct application the ideas and practices considered in the previous sections, so that the extent of their relevance and feasibility can be evaluated in the actual process of teaching. The tasks which are proposed here, with their clear specification of aims and procedures and kinds of evaluation required, are designed to enable readers to investigate the interaction that goes on in their own classrooms, and as part of teaching, to experiment with patterns of participation which might promote the purpose of learning more effectively.

The plan of the book conforms to the general pattern laid down for the scheme of the series as a whole. It is designed to engage readers in a process of task-based discovery which begins with abstract enquiry and extends into practical action.

This process is activated by a combination of inter-related text and task. In Section One, it is the text which is primary, and the tasks play a supporting role. The text expounds and explains ideas that bear upon the topic in question, and the tasks are devised to clarify these ideas by invoking the reader's own experiences of language and society. In Section Two, text and task are in reciprocal balance. The text demonstrates how pedagogic proposals and practices relate to the ideas examined in Section One, and the tasks involve readers in evaluation by drawing on their professional experience as language teachers. In Section Three, it is the tasks which are primary, and the text plays the supporting role of giving guidance as to how they relate to the matters raised in other sections of the book. The tasks here are modelled on those of Section Two, but they have a quite different function. Whereas the tasks in Section Two cast the reader in the role of critical observer of the efforts of others, the tasks in Section Three require readers to take direct action themselves. It is in this section, therefore, that the initiative shifts to the reader and the book becomes operational as a manual for continuing classroom exploration of pedagogic possibilities and, concurrently, as a means of professional development.

Ann Malamah-Thomas

Language Teaching:
A Scheme for Teacher Education

The purpose of this scheme of books is to engage language teachers in a process of continual professional development. We have designed it so as to guide teachers towards the critical appraisal of ideas and the informed application of these ideas in their own classrooms. The scheme provides the means for teachers to take the initiative themselves in pedagogic planning. The emphasis is on critical enquiry as a basis for effective action.

We believe that advances in language teaching stem from the independent efforts of teachers in their own classrooms. This independence is not brought about by imposing fixed ideas and promoting fashionable formulas. It can only occur where teachers, individually or collectively, explore principles and experiment with techniques. Our purpose is to offer guidance on how this might be achieved.

The scheme consists of three sub-series of books covering areas of enquiry and practice of immediate relevance to language teaching and learning. Sub-series 1 focuses on areas of *language knowledge*, with books linked to the conventional levels of linguistic description: pronunciation, vocabulary, grammar, and discourse. Sub-series 2 focuses on different *modes of behaviour* which realize this knowledge. It is concerned with the pedagogic skills of speaking, listening, reading, and writing. Sub-series 3 (of which this present volume forms a part) focuses on a variety of *modes of action* which are needed if this knowledge and behaviour is to be acquired in the operation of language teaching. The books in this sub-series have to do with such topics as syllabus design, the content of language courses, and aspects of methodology and evaluation.

This sub-division of the field is not meant to suggest that different topics can be dealt with in isolation. On the contrary, the concept of a scheme implies making coherent links between all these different areas of enquiry and activity. We wish to emphasize how their integration formalizes the complex factors present in any teaching process. Each book, then, highlights a particular topic, but also deals contingently with other issues, themselves treated as focal in other books in the series. Clearly, an enquiry into a mode of behaviour like speaking, for example, must also refer to aspects of language knowledge which it realizes. It must also connect to modes of action which can be directed at developing this behaviour in learners. As elements of the whole scheme, therefore, books cross-refer both within and across the different sub-series.

This principle of cross-reference which links the elements of the scheme is also applied to the internal design of the different inter-related books within it. Thus, each book contains three sections, which, by a combination of text and task, engage the reader in a principled enquiry into ideas and practices. The first section of each book makes explicit those theoretical ideas which bear on the topic in question. It provides a conceptual framework for those sections which follow. Here the text has a mainly *explanatory* function, and the tasks serve to clarify and consolidate the points raised. The second section shifts the focus of attention to how the ideas from Section One relate to activities in the classroom. Here the text is concerned with *demonstration*, and the tasks are designed to get readers to evaluate suggestions for teaching in reference both to the ideas from Section One and also to their own teaching experience. In the third section this experience is projected into future work. Here the set of tasks, modelled on those in Section Two, are designed to be carried out by the reader as a combination of teaching techniques and action research in the actual classroom. It is this section that renews the reader's contact with reality: the ideas expounded in Section One and linked to pedagogic practice in Section Two are now to be systematically *tested out* in the process of classroom teaching.

If language teaching is to be a genuinely professional enterprise, it requires continual experimentation and evaluation on the part of practitioners whereby in seeking to be more effective in their pedagogy they provide at the same time—and as a corollary—for their own continuing education. It is our aim in this scheme to promote this dual purpose.

Christopher Candlin
Henry Widdowson

Defining

1　Defining classroom interaction

1.1　Classroom action

Most classroom lessons are based on a plan. The plan may have been drawn up by the teacher, or, in lessons which closely follow a textbook, it may be the textbook writer's plan. In some cases, teacher and students may work out a plan together to determine how their next lesson is to proceed.

Teacher-trainees and teachers new to their profession will tend to prepare highly detailed lesson plans, noting every example and every exercise item to be used. More experienced teachers will perhaps make do with a more general plan, scribbled down in a few headings, or kept in their heads, memorized over years of practice in the classroom.

To have no plan at all is to risk a muddled lesson. For a lesson plan is a plan of action, and shows that the teacher knows what he or she wants to do in the lesson. If the teacher does not have a clear idea of the aim of the lesson, and if the students cannot help to determine a line of action, then nothing useful or meaningful may be achieved at all.

The success of any lesson is partly dependent on the kind of planning that has gone into it. A good plan for classroom action is a first step to success. But what precisely constitutes a 'good plan'?

 TASK 1

Here is a plan for a lesson introducing the Present Perfect tense. Study the plan and state whether you think it is a good plan, that could result in a successful lesson, or not. Give reasons for your answer, or even for your inability to provide an answer, if you feel that you are unable to judge the plan. Note these reasons down.

1　Introduce vocabulary necessary for presentation: *door, window, duster, dirty hands, comb, hair,* etc.

2　Revise tenses to be used in presentation:

It's cold.
What am I going to do? (–door)
What am I doing? *close*

Now, it's too hot.
What am I going to do? (–window)
What am I doing? *open*

Look at the board.
What am I going to do?
What am I doing? *clean*

Now look at my hands. They're very dirty.
What am I going to do?
What am I doing? *wash*

And there's chalk in my hair too.
What am I going to do?
What am I doing? *comb*

3 Introduce Present Perfect tense with same examples, i.e.

What am I going to do?
What am I doing?
Look, I have *closed the door/opened the window/cleaned the board/washed my hands/combed my hair.*

4 Get class to repeat the Present Perfect items with *you have . . .*

5 **Drill**: hold up different pictures of *washing clothes/brushing hair/combing hair/opening box/closing door/cleaning car*, etc. and ask:
What have you done?
What have I done?

6 **Game**: put class in pairs with 5/6 pictures for each pair.
A picks up picture 1:
I have washed the car today.
What have you done today?
B picks up picture 2:
I have brushed the floor today.
What have you done today?
And so on.

As a result of your work on the lesson plan above, can you compile a checklist of the sort of things you would look for in judging a lesson plan? For example:

– clear headings for different sections
– timings for each section
and so on.

1.2 Action and reaction

Having a sound plan for action is only a beginning. When the plan is put into action, things get more complicated. For action is normally followed by reaction, in the classroom as everywhere else. The teacher's plan of action, translated into action in the classroom, is bound to evoke some sort of student reaction.

Teaching is undertaken so that learning can occur. Hence the success of any lesson can best be judged in terms of the learning that results from it, in terms of the learners' reactions to the teacher's action.

If a teacher knows a class well, he or she may be able to predict student reaction to the different activities to be used in the classroom, although human reaction can sometimes be quite unpredictable and unexpected. If a teacher is more preoccupied with teaching than with learning, he or she may take student reactions for granted, and not trouble to predict what they might be, or find out what they really are as they occur in the course of a lesson. What can happen if a teacher does not take this trouble?

 ## TASK 2

Here is the lesson plan from Task 1 translated into action in a classroom, and a note of the class reactions alongside the relevant parts of the plan. Study this outline of Teacher Action and Class Reaction, and state whether you think this is a successful lesson or not. Give reasons for your answer, or even for your inability to provide an answer, and note these reasons down.

Lesson plan	Class reaction
1 Vocabulary introduction through translation/ paraphrasing	Silence
2 Revision of *going-to*/ Pres. Continuous tenses	Most of class have problems with the *going-to* future. They reply 'You are going to the door', 'You are going to the board', etc. And some extend it to 'You are going to the wash', 'You are going to the comb'.
3 Presentation	Silence
4 Repetition of Present Perfect items	The class clearly have not heard the final 'd' sound of the past participle. They all chant, 'You have close the door', 'You have wash your hands', etc.

5 Drill with pictures	The class continue the above error into the drill. No final 'd' sound can be heard on any of the past participles.
6 Game in pairs with pictures	The class do not understand the teacher's instruction for this game. Confused, they end up sitting talking about the pictures in their native tongue, while the teacher sits at the front marking homework.

Now look at the different class reactions, and state which ones you think:

1 could/should have been predicted by the teacher;
2 were quite unpredictable;
3 needed further investigation by the teacher when they occurred.

Apart from making better predictions of the class's reactions, what could this teacher have done to make the lesson more successful?

1.3 Classroom interaction

Action and reaction are not interaction. The progress of the lesson outlined above is shown in Figure 1.

Teacher   Class

Figure 1

The teacher follows his plan of action and acts, according to plan, upon the class. He gets them to repeat, makes them do exercises, organizes them for a game-type activity. The class react to the teacher's actions in different ways. They repeat some things well, some things badly; they give some answers correctly, and make mistakes with others; they follow the teacher's instructions with some activities, and fail to do so with others; at times they sit silently, demonstrating no apparent reaction.

The teacher, however, fails to respond to these reactions. He does not probe the silence to see if it indicates understanding or confusion. He does not pick up the mistakes to see how he can iron them out. He does not notice the confusion when he leaves the students to work in pairs. He forges ahead with his prepared plan of action regardless of class reaction, and he seems to be acting in complete isolation from the class.

Interaction is more than this, more than action followed by reaction. Interaction means acting reciprocally, acting upon each other. Thus a lesson which exemplified interaction would progress as shown in Figure 2.

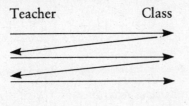

Figure 2

The teacher acts upon the class, but the class reaction subsequently modifies his next action, and so on. The class reaction becomes in itself an action, evoking a reaction in the teacher, which influences his subsequent action. There is a constant pattern of mutual influence and adjustment. How does this work out in practice in the classroom?

 TASK 3

Here is the same lesson plan from Task 1 being put into action in another classroom. Compare the progress of the lesson here with that of the lesson outlined in Task 2. Where are the main points of difference?

The teacher introduces the new vocabulary through a mixture of pictures, mime, and real objects. She asks the class for a translation of each vocabulary item into their native tongue. She then launches into her revision of the other tenses necessary for her presentation of the Present Perfect, quickly realizing that the class has problems with the *going-to* future. She immediately cuts out this tense, deciding to do her presentation on the basis of the Present Continuous alone:

> *I am opening the door*
> *I have opened the door*

and makes a mental note to do some thorough *going-to* revision in the near future. She presents her Present Perfect examples, asking the class for a quick translation of two or three of them before moving on to the repetition drill. A few of the learners, she notices, are looking a bit confused during her presentation. When she moves into the repetition phase, she immediately realizes that most of the class are leaving off the final 'd' sound.

> *I have close the window.*

So she does some pronunciation work, an ear-training exercise in recognizing the difference between *close* and *closed*, *wash* and *washed*, and so on, followed by some production work in both forms. After ten minutes of this, she is ready to go back to the repetition of the original Present Perfect items, and this time the class repeat them perfectly. She realizes, however, that she has time now to do only the picture drill, and that she had better leave the pair-work activity she had planned until another lesson.

In what way(s) can this lesson be said to exemplify classroom interaction between teacher and class?

1.4 Co-operation and conflict

Interaction is a two-way process. It can proceed harmoniously, as in the lesson scenario in Task 3 above, or it can be fraught with tensions. It can be a positive state, where the interactants feel that something worthwhile is being achieved as a result of the interaction, or it can be a negative one. Every interaction situation has the potential for co-operation or conflict. How the situation actually develops depends on the attitudes and intentions of the people involved, and on their interpretations of each other's attitudes and intentions.

For example, here is a lesson plan aimed at bringing about a co-operative atmosphere in a classroom. The teacher is a young man, with several years' experience of teaching in his own country, who has just secured a job overseas. He is taking his first class, an evening class of about sixteen adults, who all did some English at school, but who now want to improve their reading skills in English for both career and leisure purposes. The new teacher is keen to establish a strong feeling of group solidarity in the class and good student–teacher relationships.

Lesson plan

1 *Relaxation*: eyes closed for three minutes.

2 *How much do we know about each other?*
   The Label game: each student has six sticky labels and writes a different adjective on each, for example *clever, clumsy, witty, nice, ambitious*, etc. Students then circulate, sticking their adjectives on to the jackets of classmates they most appropriately fit.

3 *Discussion*: how each student felt when different adjectives were attached to him, which adjectives each student would have liked to have attached to him, which adjectives each student would not have liked attached to him, and so on.

▶ TASK 4

Given that the class members are all middle-aged, reserved, and very conscientious about improving their English; that their previous experience of language learning has been of doing grammar and comprehension exercises and of memorizing vocabulary lists, what reaction to this lesson plan can you predict?

Now look at the interaction which might arise from the execution of this lesson plan:

Teacher	Class
1 Let's see how they take to relaxing . . .	What is this man doing? We're here to learn English, not to relax. I don't understand. Is this some new method?
Mmm. They don't seem too too happy. Perhaps I'd better explain more fully the importance of relaxation for a friendly atmosphere . . .	We were all quite relaxed before. I don't know why he's wasting time like this!
2 OK. I'd better get on with the Label game, and let them see the point of my approach . . .	Aha! A vocabulary exercise, good. We write adjectives . . . but why on labels? We'll soon see . . .
They seem happy, but they think this is just a language exercise. I'll explain what they are to do with the labels . . .	My goodness. He can't be serious. *Clever, witty* . . . all right. But who shall I stick *bad-tempered* or *nasty* on to? And what shall I do if anyone puts a bad adjective on me?
They don't like it. They're afraid. But they have to be honest with each other if we are to get a good class atmosphere going . . .	He can't force us to play this ridiculous game. But perhaps a few adjectives will humour him . . .
That's better. They're playing the game. If I encourage them, they might get into the spirit of things and use the bad adjectives too . . .	This is ridiculous! We are here to learn English, not insult each other. This young man needs a lesson . . . oh look, Frau Schmidt is going up to him with a label.

Good. Frau Schmidt is coming to me with a label. What is it? *Stupid*. She's stuck *stupid* on me.

Stupid! Good for her. Serves him right. She's told him what she thinks of him.

My God. Is she being rude? A fine way to welcome a new teacher. What a cheek!

Oh dear. He's gone red. Maybe she shouldn't have done that. But he did ask for it, making us do such stupid things.

The interaction has developed into conflict. The classroom atmosphere by this stage is fraught with tension, and it is difficult to see how the lesson can progress from here. Could this conflict have been avoided?

 ## TASK 5

Suggest ways in which the above lesson might have taken a more co-operative path. This might involve changes in the actual lesson plan as well as in the execution of it.

Can the situation be repaired?

 ## TASK 6

If you were the teacher of the above lesson in this situation, what would/could you do now to set the lesson on a more co-operative path?

1.5 Communication

▶ TASK 7

Of the three lessons outlined above, the two different Present Perfect lessons (in Tasks 2 and 3) and the one aimed at creating good classroom relations (Task 4), which lesson do you think provided most opportunity for learning? Give reasons for your choice. Why was there less opportunity for learning in the other two lessons?

Having a plan of action means that the teacher knows what he or she wants to do in the classroom. The teacher has something to communicate to the students.

But having something to communicate is not the same thing as actually communicating it. In order to achieve this, the plan of action must be carried out in a context of interaction. The teacher must engage in the sort of interaction with the learners which will enable communication to take place.

Where there is no interaction, but only action and reaction, there can be no communication. Where there is conflict in the interaction, communication breaks down. Only where there is co-operation between both sides involved in the interaction can communication effectively take place, and learning occur.

Knowing what you want to do, what you want to communicate to your students, in the classroom is a good start. Actually doing it, actually achieving communication, requires a lot more effort and expertise.

2 Defining communication in the classroom

2.1 Who

Communication implies more than one person. There must be someone to transmit a message, and someone to receive it. The average classroom contains between twenty and sixty people. There are, therefore, any number of possible variations on who does the transmitting and who does the receiving.

If we take the teacher as the one transmitting a message, then he or she can be seen as trying to communicate with the whole class, a group of students, or an individual student at different points of the lesson. In the preceding sections, interaction between the teacher and the whole class was stressed, but there are clearly activities where the teacher is a participant in interaction with an individual student, or with a group of students within the class.

▶ TASK 8

Can you give examples of different activities where the teacher is engaged in interaction with (1) a group of students, and (2) an individual student?

And what about the student's role in the classroom interaction?

▶ TASK 9

Now take an individual student as the one transmitting a message, and work out the various combinations that he or she can be seen as communicating in:

S ⟶
S ⟶
S ⟶
S ⟶

Then give examples of the sort of activity that would engage the student in each different pattern of interaction, for example:

S ⟶ individual student in pair-work, group-work, informal chat, etc.

Teacher and students are not the only participants in classroom interaction. In many classrooms, lessons closely follow procedures laid down in a textbook. In such cases, the textbook writer can be seen as the transmitter of a message, communicating indirectly with the teacher and students in the classroom. For example:

Textbook writer ————————➤ teacher and whole class, when they are all doing an exercise in the book together, orally.

Textbook writer ————————➤ teacher, when he or she is adapting an exercise from the book to give the class at a later date.

▶ TASK 10

Now work out what the situation would be when the textbook writer is communicating with

an individual student
a group of students.

Teacher, students, and textbook writers are thus the participants in classroom interaction. They communicate with each other in various different combinations. And they communicate with each other in very different ways, teacher and students being in a much more direct and clearly apparent relationship.

The identity of these participants is crucial to any communication they undertake. People communicate most easily with those they have most in common with. When they have little in common with each other, they communicate only with difficulty. A teacher with the same sort of background and experience as his or her students will have a good chance of communicating with them. A teacher with very different background and experience has to try to learn as much as possible about the students, and they must also try to make allowance for the teacher, before communication can take place. Otherwise, problems can occur.

▶ TASK 11

Try to explain the problems in the lesson outlined in Task 4 in Unit 1 in terms of differences of experience and expectations between teacher and learners.

Similarly, a textbook writer will communicate more easily with the teachers and students for whom the book is written if he or she shares, or is at least aware of, their particular experience and expectations of classroom learning and teaching.

2.2 Why

Communication is undertaken for a purpose. There is always a reason for transmitting a message to someone else. The classroom situation, like many other social situations, involves gathering people together for a specific purpose: in this case, the purpose of learning.

The primary purpose of classroom communication is a pedagogic one. The teacher is in command of a body of knowledge and of skills that he or she is required to transmit to the learners. In the language classroom, the teacher knows the language; the learners do not.

The learners, inasmuch as they are speakers of their native language and of any other languages, know something about language and the way it works in general. If they have formally learned any other language, they also know something about language learning. There is thus sufficient common ground for teacher–learner interaction to take place with the purpose of learning the new language.

A teacher's pedagogic reasons for undertaking communication in the classroom are fairly clear: to present a new structure; to provide the learners with practice in using that structure; to explain a new word; to provide a model for pronunciation; to correct an error, and so on. But what about the students? What reasons does the learner have for communication in the classroom?

► TASK 12

Think of at least five pedagogic reasons (i.e. reasons connected with the learning of the new language) that the student might have for communicating a message in the classroom to:

the teacher
another student
a group of students.

Although learning is the focus of classroom communication, not all of the latter is pedagogic in nature. People have other reasons for communicating in the classroom. In common with all other social settings, there is the need to establish and maintain personal relationships. The teacher has to establish a rapport with the class, and with the individuals of which the class is composed. Individual students form different sorts of relationships with each other, and take up different attitudes towards the teacher.

A teacher can set out to be harsh, strict, and authoritarian with a class; or kind, tolerant, and permissive. He or she can remain at a formal distance from the students, or become involved with all of them—their personal lives, their hopes, and their problems.

Similarly, students can adopt different attitudes in the classroom.

► TASK 13

Looking at the student–teacher relationship, can you say what sorts of attitudes individual students might develop towards their teacher?

And looking at the student–student relationship, can you say what sorts of attitudes individual students might develop towards their classmates?

Another reason for classroom communication stems from the formal nature of the classroom situation itself, and the need to organize it for learning purposes. Attendance registers have to be taken, books given out or taken in, furniture arranged to facilitate teaching and learning activities, and so on. Much classroom communication therefore centres on organization and administration, matters necessary to the learning process, but not directly pedagogic in themselves.

► TASK 14

Give some examples of organizational or administrative reasons for the following types of communication:

1 teacher ⟶ whole class
2 teacher ⟶ group of students
3 teacher ⟶ individual student
4 student ⟶ teacher
5 student ⟶ student
6 student ⟶ group of students.

2.3 What

The content of communication, the actual message being transmitted, is closely linked to the purpose of communication. Thus, in a language classroom, communication with a pedagogic purpose will have a strictly pedagogic content: information about the grammar or the use of the language; information about how linguistic skills, such as those of reading or listening, operate in that particular language; information about the speakers of the language and the culture they adhere to. This can be termed the *classroom transaction*, the communication of information, and is clearly in the control of the teacher, or the textbook writer, the possessor of the information.

When it comes to communication for more personal purposes, this can be seen as the *classroom interaction*, the establishment of rapport and a sense of community. The content of the messages being transmitted here is of a very different nature.

▶ ## TASK 15

Below are three examples of the sort of interpersonal message that a teacher might try to transmit in a classroom.

- I am in control. If you disobey me, you will be punished.
- I am very clever. Much cleverer than all of you students.
- I am a kind person, and I am interested in all of you as individuals.

Think back to teachers you had in your school days and write down the messages you think they were trying to transmit about themselves. Then think about five or six students you have known, and write down the interpersonal messages they were transmitting in the classroom about themselves.

It is personal interaction of this kind that is responsible for the overall classroom atmosphere, or ambience. Clearly, the teacher can do much towards creating a positive atmosphere, but the influence of the learners and their attitudes is equally important. The particular interplay of personalities in any one classroom can often produce quite unpredictable results.

The content of communication for organizational and administrative purposes refers to a fairly restricted area of interaction: taking the register, moving the furniture, setting up activities, giving out books, positioning the students, announcing school holidays, and so on. The teacher, who is traditionally given administrative control of the classroom, must be seen as the prime instigator of communication of this nature.

2.4 How

Communication is achieved by means of a variety of resources. Participants in classroom communication can draw both on language and on non-verbal resources in the same way as they can in any other social situation.

Classroom communication of an administrative or organizational nature is carried out through a mixture of language and gesture. The teacher gives orders and instructions, or makes gestures like pointing to a student and then to a pile of books to be distributed, or a blackboard to be cleaned. Sometimes, administrative or organizational matters are dealt with in written notices, or in diagrams, indicating such things as the positions to be taken by students when sitting a test or an examination.

▶ ## TASK 16

In the following examples of the content of organizational and administrative communication, what actual words, spoken or written, or what gestures or diagrams might be used by a teacher addressing students, and by students responding to the teacher?

1 Calling the register
2 Furniture moving
3 Setting up activities
4 Giving out books
5 Positioning of students
6 Announcements about dates

Interpersonal communication in the classroom is achieved by drawing on the same resources as are available in all other social situations. The way people dress, the way they move, sit, and stand, can say a great deal about their attitudes towards the people they are communicating with. Facial expressions and the tone of voice used when speaking can all say much more about how a person feels than the words that he or she actually utters. In this area of classroom communication, in fact, non-verbal resources as an instrument of communication probably play just as important a part as language does.

 ## TASK 17

Consider the following attitudes under the headings 'Teacher' and 'Student'. How would each of these attitudes be communicated through dress, posture, behaviour, facial expression, tone of voice, and use of language?

Teacher

1 Friendly, relaxed, on an equal footing with the students.
2 Strict, authoritarian, stands no nonsense from the students.
3 Very clever, too clever to be teaching these students.
4 Warm, but not too friendly, tolerant but not permissive with the students.

Student

5 Conscientious, hard-working, eager to please the teacher.
6 Hates school, dislikes authority, wants to appear a hero to the other students.
7 Very clever, knows it all, and knows more than the teacher.
8 Joker, always trying to raise a laugh from teacher or classmates.

But the one thing that makes the classroom different from any other social situation is its primary pedagogic purpose. The classroom exists so that students can learn, and the main focus of most classroom communication is a pedagogic one.

The pedagogic message is transmitted by different means. Language is an important factor in pedagogic communication and teachers spend a lot of time talking, lecturing, asking questions, giving definitions, reading aloud, giving instructions, and so on. Students answer the questions, repeat or write down what they hear in lectures and instructions, talk to each other in activities and projects set up by the teacher.

But language is not the only means of communicating the pedagogic messages of the classroom. The teacher can use demonstration or mime, can draw pictures or show pictures of a still or moving variety. He or she can employ diagrams and charts, or use specially developed gestures, to get the message across. Good teaching, in fact, involves using a variety of resources and knowing which to use in order to communicate a message most effectively.

2.5 Methodology and language

Classroom communication of a social nature, with a personal or organizational purpose, draws on language as one of its available resources. So does classroom communication with a pedagogic purpose. But the language is used very differently in each case.

If the teacher asks a student, 'What did you do last night?' in an attempt to establish friendly relations with the student and find out more about his personal life, then she is genuinely interested in the content of the answer. If she asks the same question in the context of an exercise on the Past Simple tense, with a pedagogic purpose, she is interested only in whether the student can produce the correct form of the verb, *I went* or *I watched* or *I did*, or whatever.

Similarly, if a teacher tells a group of students, 'Move these two desks together, and then put those chairs on top', with an organizational purpose, he really wants the furniture moved. If he gives the same instructions as part of a listening comprehension exercise, he is interested only in whether the students understand him or not, and can carry out his instructions precisely.

In the first case in each example, we have language used conventionally to achieve a social purpose. In the second case, we have language used as a methodological device to achieve a pedagogic purpose. The Simple Past tense is elicited by asking a question; it could have been elicited by showing a picture, or performing a mime, with a gesture of pointing over the shoulder to indicate 'last night' or 'yesterday'. Listening comprehension is tested by referring to furniture in the immediate classroom situation; it could have been tested by referring to wooden blocks on the students' desks, to pictures in the students' books, to a diagram on the blackboard.

In the language classroom, where the pedagogic purpose of communication is inherently linguistic in nature, the social and pedagogic purposes are often conflated. For example, a teacher may really want the furniture moved, but may choose to give the furniture-moving instructions in the target language so as to provide some listening practice for the students at the same time. The teacher's instructions are thus simultaneously a means for achieving a social purpose and a methodological device to achieve a pedagogic one.

▶ **TASK 18**

Indicate for each of the following whether you think it is
a a linguistic device for a social (personal, organizational) purpose;
b a methodological device for a pedagogic purpose;
c possibly both together.

1 *Where's Mary today? Is she ill?*
2 *When was the Battle of Hastings?*
3 Talking about being punctual for school.
4 Talking about the uses of the Present Perfect tense.
5 Instructions on how to get from the school to the Post Office.
6 *What's your favourite food?*
7 *When are the Easter holidays?*
8 Instructions on how to repair a bicycle puncture.
9 *If you do that again, you'll be sorry.*
10 Directions to the Head teacher's office.

Language is a primary resource for social communication between teacher and students, and vice versa. Methodology is the resource for pedagogic communication between teacher and class. The methodological device employed can be verbal in nature, but can equally well be of a pictorial or other non-verbal variety.

3 Defining interaction analysis

The preceding Units have built up a picture of the very complex web of interrelationships and interactions that go to make up a classroom lesson. When the complexity of what goes on in the classroom is fully realized, it can be seen how difficult it is to produce an accurate description or analysis of the teaching and learning processes in any lesson. Classroom-based research over the last twenty years has produced a variety of models, operating from a variety of viewpoints, for describing and analysing interaction in the classroom.

3.1 Interaction analysis

The basis of the 'interaction analysis' tradition, established with Flanders' categories of description for classroom verbal behaviour (1970), is to look at classroom language to see what it can reveal about the teaching and learning processes. Use of language is, after all, highly observable, whereas learning is not.

Moreover, in Western culture at least, language is widely used for pedagogic purposes. Talking is almost equated with teaching in many situations. There is, therefore, a large amount of language use to observe, particularly on the teacher's part.

There are in existence many hundreds of classroom observation instruments in this tradition. All of them are essentially adaptations, extensions, or simplifications of Flanders' original categories. These comprise two main categories, *teacher talk* and *pupil talk*, with a third category to cover other types of verbal behaviour, or lack of it.

▶ TASK 19

Here are the ten original Flanders' Interaction Analysis Categories (FIAC). Study them to see what they can tell the observer about the communication going on in any classroom in terms of the *who*, *why*, *what*, and *how* outlined above. Also, what aspects of classroom communication will they fail to reveal?

Teacher talk
1 **Accepts feeling:** Accepts and clarifies an attitude or the feeling tone of a pupil in a non-threatening manner. Feelings may be positive or negative. Predicting and recalling feelings are included.

2 **Praises or encourages**: Praises or encourages pupil action or behaviour. Makes jokes that release tension, but not at the expense of another individual. Nodding head or saying 'Um hm?' or 'Go on' are included.

3 **Accepts or uses ideas of pupils**: Clarifying, building, or developing ideas suggested by a pupil. Teacher extensions of pupil ideas are included, but as the teacher brings more of his or her own ideas into play, shift to category five.

4 **Asks questions**: Asking a question about content or procedure, based on teacher ideas, with the intent that a pupil will answer.

5 **Lecturing**: Giving facts or opinions about content or procedures; expressing own ideas, giving own explanation, or citing an authority other than a pupil.

6 **Giving directions**: Directions, commands, or orders with which a pupil is expected to comply.

7 **Criticizing or justifying authority**: Statements intended to change pupil behaviour from non-acceptable to acceptable pattern; bawling someone out; stating why the teacher is doing what he or she is doing; extreme self-reference.

Pupil talk

8 **Pupil talk: response**: Talk by pupils in response to teacher. Teacher initiates the contact, or solicits pupil statement, or structures the situation. Freedom to express own ideas is limited.

9 **Pupil talk: initiation**: Talk by pupils which they initiate. Expressing own ideas; initiating a new topic; freedom to develop opinions and a line of thought, like asking thoughtful questions; going beyond the existing structure.

Silence

10 **Silence or confusion**: Pauses, short periods of silence and periods of confusion in which communication cannot be understood by the observer.

An observer coding a classroom lesson according to FIAC will end up with an analysis along the following lines (the mechanics of observation and coding are dealt with in Section Two of this book):

Category 5: Teacher lectures   90% of lesson
Category 4: Teacher asks questions 3% of lesson
Category 8: Pupil response   3% of lesson
Category 10: Silence   4% of lesson

▶   TASK 20

What exactly does this analysis tell you about the lesson observed? Consider the categories excluded as well as those included: the proportion of time taken by each category; the amount of teacher talk compared to the amount of pupil talk, and so on.

Can you form any judgements on the success of the lesson analysed here? If so, on what evidence do you base your judgements? If not, why not?

Whether it tells us what we want to know or not, the aim of observing classroom language use like this is to find out about the teaching and learning that goes on in a classroom. As such it is to be differentiated from observing classroom language in order to find out more about how language works. The former is an educational aim, the latter a linguistic one.

Classroom language was used as the raw data for linguistic research with this latter aim in view by Sinclair and Coulthard (1975) in their work on discourse analysis. Classroom language, they felt, provided a relatively simple and more structured type of discourse than normal everyday conversation with all its unpredictabilities and ambiguities.

The result of their work is a descriptive system (see Section Two) which can be used to analyse the verbal interaction in a classroom. It is not, however, designed to throw light on the teaching and learning interaction as such.

3.2 Interaction analysis in the language classroom

The tradition of interaction analysis described above was carried over into the language-teaching classroom soon after it was established in the early 1970s. An instrument directly inspired by FIAC was Moskowitz's FLINT (Foreign Language Interaction) (see Moskowitz 1976). This takes Flanders' original categories, but with several adaptations and additions to make them more relevant to practice in the language classroom. Here for example is the FLINT extension of Flanders' two *pupil-talk* categories, Response and Initiation (the letters indicate sub-divisions of the categories):

Student talk
8   Specific: Responding to the teacher within a specific and limited range of available or previously shaped answers.
8a Choral: Choral response by the total class or part of the class.
8r Reads Orally: A student or students read aloud to the class.

9   Open-ended or Student-Initiated: Responding to the teacher with students' own ideas, opinions, reactions, feelings: giving one from

among many possible answers which have been previously shaped but from which students must now make a selection. Initiating the participation.

9a Off Task: Acting fresh. Being off the subject and non-task-oriented. Being disorderly. This category refers to individual students.

 ## TASK 21

Study the five FLINT *student-talk* categories above. Indicate whether each one serves to describe:

a. communication for a strictly pedagogic purpose;
b. communication for a social (personal/organizational) purpose;
c. possibly both of the above.

By looking at classroom language, FLINT, like FIAC, records information about both the pedagogic and the social aspects of classroom interaction, since language is used for both. This comes out even more clearly in the *teacher-talk* sections, where the categories cover both methodological uses of language (focusing on the teaching and learning process) and social, personal, and organizational uses of language (which serve to facilitate the teaching and learning process).

TASK 22

Now study the various categories in the *teacher-talk* section of FLINT listed below, and indicate whether each describes:

a. communication for a pedagogic purpose focal to teaching and learning;
b. communication for a social (personal/organizational) purpose to facilitate teaching and learning;
c. possibly both of the above.

Teacher talk

Indirect influence

1 **Deals with feelings**: in a non-threatening way, accepting, reflecting, discussing, referring to, identifying with or communicating understanding of past, present, or future feelings of students.

2 **Praises or encourages**: praising, complimenting, telling students why what they have said or done is valued. Encouraging students to continue, trying to give them confidence. Confirming that answers are correct.

2a **Jokes**: intentional joking, kidding, making puns: attempting to be humorous, providing the joking is not at anyone's expense.

3   **Uses ideas of students**: clarifying, using, interpreting, summarizing the ideas of students. The ideas must be rephrased by the teacher but still recognized as being students' contributions.

3a **Repeats student response verbatim**: repeating the exact words of students after they participate. This often occurs in a pattern drill.

4   **Asks questions**: asking questions to which an answer is expected. (Rhetorical questions are not included in this category.)

4c **Asks cultural questions**: asking questions related to the culture and civilization of the target people or country.

4p **Personalizes**: asking questions which relate to the students' personal lives. Relating the content being learned to the students' personal lives. Relating the content being learned to the students themselves through personal qualities.

Direct influence

5   **Gives information**: giving information, facts, own opinions or ideas, lecturing, or asking rhetorical questions.

5a **Corrects without rejection**: telling students who have made a mistake the correct response without using words or intonations which communicate criticism.

5c **Discusses culture and civilization**: talking about the culture and civilization of the target people or country. Presenting facts, anecdotes, points of interest related to the cultural aspect.

5m **Models**: modelling examples for students. Giving the lines of a dialogue, a sample for a pattern drill, illustrating the pronunciation of words or sounds.

5o **Orients**: telling students the procedures they will be following. Giving an overview or preview of what is to come. Setting standards, regulations, or expectations.

5p **Personalizes about self**: talking about himself (herself). Telling a personal story or anecdote about his (her) life.

5r **Carries out routine tasks**: attending to routine matters, i.e. taking attendance, passing out books, test papers, etc. Making routine announcements.

6   **Gives directions**: giving directions, requests, or commands which students are expected to follow.

6a **Directs pattern drills**: giving statements which students are expected to repeat exactly, to make substitutions in (i.e. substitution drills), or to change from one form to another (i.e. transformation drills).

7   **Criticizes student behaviour**: rejecting the behaviour of students, trying to change the non-acceptable behaviour. Communicates anger, displeasure, annoyance or dissatisfaction with what students are doing.

7a **Criticizes student response**: telling the student his response is not correct or acceptable and communicating by words or intonation criticism, displeasure, annoyance, rejection.

3.3 Analysing language in the language classroom

A more recent, and less cumbersome, instrument in the interaction analysis tradition is Bowers' Categories of Verbal Behaviour in the Language Classroom (1980). Bowers identifies from his classroom language data seven categories of 'move' within a lesson, a 'move' being the smallest unit in his particular system of description.

His categories make far clearer than FLINT the distinction between language used directly in connection with teaching and learning, and language used for normal social or organizational purposes (although there are still some grey areas).

Responding: any act directly sought by the utterance of another speaker, such as answering a question.

Sociating: any act not contributing directly to the teaching/learning task, but rather to the establishment or maintenance of interpersonal relationships.

Organizing: any act which serves to structure the learning task or environment without contributing to the teaching/learning task itself.

Directing: any act encouraging non-verbal activity as an integral part of the teaching/learning task.

Presenting: any act presenting information of direct relevance to the learning task.

Evaluating: any act which rates another verbal act positively or negatively.

Eliciting: any act designed to produce a verbal response from another person.

 TASK 23

Study Bowers' seven categories above. Indicate whether each describes

a. communication with a pedagogic purpose;
b. communication with a social (personal/organizational) purpose;
c. possibly both of the above.

3.4 Analysing methodology in the language classroom

The interaction analysis tradition looks at verbal interaction in the classroom to understand the teaching and learning behaviour going on there. Many classroom observers have tried to set up descriptive systems looking at other features of the language classroom which are associated with this behaviour, including aspects of verbal interaction where they seem relevant.

These observers concentrate on analysing how interaction is realized as a particular classroom methodology, or set of language teaching strategies. They therefore include *topic* or *content* as a major category of description in their observation instruments. It is, after all, important to know what is to be taught and learned in any lesson and not only what kind of interaction takes place. Here are the Content/Topic categories from three different instruments of this type, with explanations where necessary of what these categories refer to. (See Section Two for more details of the instruments themselves.)

TALOS (Target Language Observation Scheme)
(see Ullman and Geva 1984)

Content focus

Linguistic: Substantive:
1 Sound   5 Grammar
2 Word   6 Culture
3 Phrase   7 Integrated subject matter.
4 Discourse

The Linguistic categories emphasize the formal properties of the target language, and cover pronunciation, vocabulary, the use of language in dialogue or text, and so on. The Substantive categories refer to overt grammar teaching, discussion of the culture of the target-language group, and any other subject matter (science, geography, history and so on) integrated with the language teaching.

COLT (Communicative Orientation of Language Teaching)
(see Ullman and Geva 1984)

Content

Management:
1 Procedure, e.g. setting up an activity
2 Discipline, e.g. reprimanding students

Language:
3 Form, e.g. grammar or pronunciation
4 Function, e.g. requests or invitations
5 Discourse, e.g. text comprehension
6 Sociolinguistic, e.g. difference between formal and informal registers

Other topics:
7 Narrow reference, e.g. classroom, personal details
8 Limited reference, e.g. family, community, school
9 Broad reference, e.g. world affairs, imagination

Mitchell and Parkinson (1979)

Topic

 1 Civilization: aspects of life and culture in the target-language country.
 2 General linguistic notions: the nature of language in general.
 3 Language points (course): structures, functions, meanings in the syllabus or coursebook.
 4 Language points (other): as above, but not included in syllabus or coursebook.
 5 Situations (course): a situation narrated or presented in the course material.
 6 Situations (other): as above, but not presented in the course.
 7 Real life: aspects of teacher's and students' lives, at home and at school.
 8 Fragmented/non-contextualized: no substantive topic.
 9 Pupil performance: previous performance of students.
10 Routine procedures: classroom organization and management.
11 Other: all other topics.

How can these different categories be applied to what goes on in the classroom?

 TASK 24

Look back to the three lesson scenarios outlined at the beginning of this section: the two lessons on the Present Perfect (in Tasks 2 and 3) and the lesson on adjectives (in Task 4). Try to analyse the topics dealt with in each lesson scenario according to the categories outlined above. One lesson, according to one instrument, has been filled in for you:

	TALOS	COLT	M + P
Lesson 1 Present Perfect (in Task 2)			
Lesson 2 Present Perfect (in Task 3)	2,5,1,5		
Lesson 3 Adjectives (in Task 4)			

As well as dealing with the *what* of classroom communication, these instruments also look at the *how*. They account for the pedagogic *activities* that the teacher employs. COLT simply requires the observer to note down the activity, be it reading aloud, dictation, drill, or whatever. TALOS and Mitchell and Parkinson specify the activities under the following categories:

TALOS

Activity Type

1 Drill
2 Dialogue
3 Frame (e.g. for a dialogue or for oral or written composition)
4 Spelling
5 Translation
6 Paraphrasing
7 Free communication (e.g. as in role play, discussion, and so on).

Mitchell and Parkinson

Language Activities

1 Interpretation: meanings of target language made explicit in native language, as in translation.
2 L1: use of native language.
3 Real FL: real messages transmitted in target language, e.g. instructions for moving furniture.
4 Transposition: focus on relationship between spoken and written word, e.g. reading aloud, dictation.
5 Presentation: focus on global comprehension, e.g. listening or reading text.
6 Imitation: students to imitate a model, e.g. repetition.
7 Drill/exercise: focus on form and/or appropriacy of utterance, e.g. structural drills, question-and-answer.
8 Compound: brief occurrences of more than one of the above in the same sequence.

Again, how can these categories be applied to what goes on in the classroom?

 TASK 25

Look back to the same three lesson scenarios that you worked on in Task 24. This time analyse the *activities* in each lesson according to the categories outlined above:

	TALOS	COLT	M + P
Lesson 1 Present Perfect			
Lesson 2 Present Perfect			
Lesson 3 Adjectives			

Now match the *topic* with the *activity* categories for each lesson. For example, Lesson 1 could be analysed according to the TALOS categories as follows:

    2 word—5 translation
            —6 paraphrasing
    5 grammar—1 drill

and so on.

Description of a lesson in these terms gives a picture of what is being taught, and which methodological device the teacher uses to teach it. But is such a description enough? Does it capture the essence of what is going on in a classroom?

▶ ## TASK 26

Do you think there are any parts of the three lessons you analysed that these categories cannot cater for?

Does analysis of lessons in these terms give you an indication of the relative success of the lessons analysed? For example, can you tell from your analysis of the three lessons above that any one is more successful than the others, and if so, why it is more successful?

Of the three systems, which did you find easiest to use, in that you could find the appropriate category of description most quickly? Which did you find most difficult to use?

3.5 Analysing affect in the language classroom

The way that participants in classroom interaction feel about each other, and about the situation they are in, has an important influence on what actually goes on in a classroom. Feelings and attitudes can make for smooth interaction and successful learning, or can lead to conflict and the total breakdown of communication.

These affective factors which operate with great influence in any classroom are probably the most difficult to describe or analyse in any objective sort of way. Moskowitz's FLINT (see 3.2 above) attempts to account for some of them. There is, for example, in addition to the categories outlined above, a category:

12n   **Teacher smiles**: the teacher is smiling very apparently and may or may not be speaking at the time.

and another category:

12   **Laughter**: laughing or giggling by the class, individuals, and/or the teacher.

TASK 27

Look back at the FLINT *teacher-talk* categories in Task 22 above. Pick out any other categories that seem relevant to the interpersonal aspects of classroom interaction, the sort of feelings the teacher can create in the classroom through his or her own behaviour.

Information can normally be gathered in a more subjective and impressionistic way about the affective factors of any classroom situation. Students can be interviewed about how they feel towards a particular teacher and his subject. Observers can absorb global impressions of classroom atmosphere, and add these to information about the physical setting created by a teacher in his own classroom through the use of pictures, charts, and other decorations; about the physical appearance and posture of the teacher himself; and about his actual behaviour during the course of a lesson.

▶ TASK 28

Think back to your own school-days. Which classroom did you enjoy being in most? Can you analyse the reasons for your choice? And which classroom did you enjoy least? Again, can you analyse the reasons for this?

3.6 The parts . . . and the whole

▶ TASK 29

Of the three areas outlined above (classroom language, classroom methodology, and classroom affect), which do you think would be the most profitable area for research? Which might tell us most about what sort of teaching and learning is going on in a classroom?

A great deal of work has gone into attempts to analyse the classroom situation. Just *how* much work will become more apparent in Section Two of this book, when the various observation schemes referred to above are treated in more detail.

The various systems of description can provide a precise and detailed picture, a neat analysis, of what goes on in many different classrooms. There is, however, no system which can be generally applied to any classroom, anywhere in the world. For each system assumes the context it was devised in, and, being based on the sort of classroom practice carried out in certain specific contexts, is, as a result, applicable only in similar contexts. This is obvious in all of the instruments described above.

► TASK 30

Look again at FLINT in 3.2, and the two other categories in 3.5. What are the assumptions about classroom practice on which FLINT is based? What sort of classroom lessons can it be used to describe? And what sort of lessons can it never apply to?

Moreover, these systems tend to concentrate on the various parts of the lesson. In order to analyse, they must fragment. And, in stressing the parts, they all overlook the whole; the whole lesson which is greater than the sum of its parts. For the crux of any classroom lesson lies in the learning that occurs in it. The crucial factor is whether the teacher gets his or her message across, whether the students learn what the teacher sets out to teach them. Any worthwhile analysis of classroom interaction must focus on this factor, and should also point up why the lesson succeeds, if it is successful, and why it fails, if it is unsuccessful.

4　Defining communicative events in the classroom

4.1　The speech event

Classroom language is used for communication purposes between teacher and students (and, in a more indirect way, between the students and the textbook writer). Like all language used for communicative purposes, it occurs in a context. Context can be broken down into different factors:

addresser:　a person trying to transmit a message

purpose:　the addresser's reason for transmitting the message

addressee:　the person to whom the message is being transmitted

content:　what the message is about

form:　how the message is delivered, the actual form of words

medium:　the medium of delivery, spoken or written

setting:　the place and the time

code:　the language in which the message is delivered, English, French or whatever.

These are the factors of the speech event (see Hymes 1962), an instance of communication drawing on the resources of language. Other types of communicative event might employ non-verbal codes, such as flowers, smoke signals, morse code, gestures, facial expressions, and so on.

These factors aim to account for the variables in any speech event. They explain *who* says *what* to *whom* and *why*, *where*, *when*, and *how*.

The addresser, given a code, has to take all these variables into account in choosing a form that will convey her message most effectively in the situation and thus achieve her purpose.

 TASK 31

Look at the following speech-event factors, and decide what form of words would be used in this particular context:

addresser: Yourself

purpose: To get silence in your class.

addressee: A boy in your class who always creates discipline problems.

content:	That the boy should stop laughing and talking with his classmates and listen to you.
medium:	Speech
setting:	Middle of English lesson on a Friday afternoon. You are reading a text out loud to a class of 15-year-old boys.
code:	Your native language.
form:	....

All of the factors are closely interrelated. A small change in one will dictate changes elsewhere. A different setting can change the other factors, as can a different purpose. All kinds of combinations of the various factors are possible.

 ## TASK 32

Take the same speech-event factors above, but change the *addressee* to a group of boys talking and laughing together. Does this change the *form* of words in any way?

Then change the *setting* to Monday morning: the beginning of a one-hour written test with the same class of boys.

Does this change any of the other factors, such as *addressee*, *content*, *medium*, and *form*?

Finally change the *purpose*: to get a boy who created discipline problems away from the friends he is talking and laughing with. What factors does this change, and how?

 ## TASK 33

Now look at things the other way round. Try to work out how the other factors of the speech event might relate to the following *form* of words:

1 'Page 10. Exercise 6. Numbers 1–5. For Monday please.'
2 'Do you know of anything worthwhile to read on the communicative approach?'

4.2 The learning event

Classroom methodology is also used for communication purposes. It is used for the transmission of the pedagogic message from teacher to student. It is the way the teacher gets his or her teaching message across. The context in which this sort of communication occurs can be broken down into the same factors as the speech event.

addresser: teacher

purpose: teaching aim/objective

addressee: student/learner

content: syllabus item/teaching point

form: activity techniques/methodological device

medium: verbal (spoken/written)/non-verbal
(pictures/mime/demonstration, etc.)

setting: classroom setting

code: methodology

The factors on the right-hand side can be seen as the factors of the learning event, on a parallel with the factors of the speech event. For every individual learning event, in a communicative view of teaching and learning, gives value to the same sort of variables as does the speech event. These factors explain who teaches what to whom and why, where, when, and how.

Given a reasonable command of methodology, the teacher, like the addresser, has a message to get across. He has a teaching objective, a definite purpose in getting it across to the learners. He has to choose a form of activity which will convey his teaching point most effectively in his situation and thus achieve his objective. He can use both verbal and non-verbal media. The particular classroom setting will affect his choice of form, depending on the physical conditions and resources, and the particular time of day, week, and academic year at which the learning event in question occurs.

▶ TASK 34

Look at the following learning-event factors, and decide what form of activities would be used in this particular context:

Teacher: Yourself

Teaching objective: To get the class to understand the use of numbers 1–10 in English, and to use these numbers appropriately themselves.

Learners: A class of forty children aged six–seven.

Syllabus item: Numbers 1–10.

Medium: Verbal (spoken); non-verbal (objects and drawings).

Setting: A poorly-resourced African primary school. Late-morning lesson in the hot season.

Code: Language-teaching methodology.

Activities:

TASK 35

Notice the differences made by a change in any of the learning-event factors.

1 In the learning event outlined above, change *learners* to a group of nine or ten adults, and *setting* to a European evening institute.

Does this change the form of activities? Does it change the teaching objective?

2 Now change *teaching objective* to understanding and use of the written forms of the numbers 1–10.

Does this change the form of *activities*?

3 Change *setting* to a well-resourced European primary school.

Does this change the form of activities?

4 And change learners to a class of twelve blind African primary-school children.

How does this change the form of activities?

▶ **TASK 36**

Now try looking at things the other way round. Study the three scenarios given at the beginning of Section One again, and note down the relevant learning-event factors for each lesson:

    a. teacher   e. medium
    b. learners   f. setting
    c. teaching objective g. code
    d. teaching point   h. activities

How far do you think the factors are properly matched? Try changing these factors, as you did in Task 35.

4.3 Accessible and acceptable

The addresser in the speech event has to choose a form of words that makes his or her intentions clear. The message must be accessible to the addressee. Thus, a shared knowledge of the code being used is essential to the participants in any communication situation.

Even with a shared knowledge of the code, misunderstandings or requests for clarification often occur in the course of verbal communication. It may not always be entirely clear to the addressee what the addresser's intentions are. This can happen in the classroom.

TASK 37

Look at the speech event outlined in Task 31. If the teacher chose to achieve his or her purpose by using the form 'What are you laughing at, boy?', this could be interpreted in two ways by the boy in question. What are the two possible interpretations?

The teacher in the learning event is faced with the same problem. She has to make her message accessible to the learners. If the learners do not see what she is trying to achieve, then there is very little chance of achieving it.

▶ TASK 38

Look back at the lesson on labels and adjectives (in Task 4). What is the teacher's objective in this lesson? Is the intention accessible to the learners? Why not? What do the learners think the teacher is trying to do?

Clearly, there is very little chance of a shared code in the classroom in the sense of learners knowing as much methodology as their teachers. Nor, in the nature of things, do learners often stop teachers in the classroom with requests for clarification:

'What exactly was that exercise all about?'
'What did you intend us to learn from this morning's lesson?'

In time, learners do begin to understand why they do what they do in a particular classroom. Exposure to different activities over a period of time enables learners to see the purpose of the activities. Moreover, in the language classroom, if activities bear some relation to linguistic activities in real life, learners will understand their intention. A reading exercise to achieve some purpose, such as extracting information for subsequent action, will make more sense than simply reading to answer some unspecified questions that the teacher will ask after they have finished.

But in the final analysis, there is a case for less mystique about methodology. The teacher could make his purpose plain by explaining to the learners why he employs certain activities. This can avoid many problems in the classroom.

But even if the addresser in the speech event manages to make a message accessible, it may not always be acceptable. The addressee may understand the intentions, but not be very happy about them, or the way they are couched. Thus when we choose a form of words, we are usually careful not to be rude or give offence to our addressee. We observe social rules of status and formality in making our message as acceptable as possible. This applies in the classroom as in any other social situation. The teacher may be able to make the teaching objective clear, but the learners still may not be able to accept it. It may be accessible, but unacceptable. The learners may feel offended in some way by the form of activities employed. They may judge the activities to be inappropriate for their needs or to their status. They may see the teaching point, but not like it, or not like the way in which it is put across.

▶ TASK 39

Look at the lesson on adjectives again. How could the teacher have made the message more accessible or more acceptable to the learners?

▶ TASK 40

There is a school of thought in methodology that claims the interpretation of lyric poetry is a good method for teaching the interpretation of normal linguistic discourse. A teacher who is convinced by this goes into a class of undergraduate engineers and presents them with a short lyric poem to work on. What reaction can she expect? Why? What can she do to prevent or counter this reaction?

4.4 Verbal interaction

Factors of the speech event define the context for verbal communication, but verbal interaction is a continuous, shifting process in which the context and its constituent factors change from second to second. In normal everyday verbal interaction, addresser and addressee are constantly changing roles. The addresser of one minute is the addressee of the next, and *vice versa*. Purpose and content change as the interaction progresses. Even setting may change, as time moves on and the participants perhaps move from one place to another.

To return to Figure 1 in 1.3 above, interaction can be seen as a process of mutual accommodation, with the addresser acting upon the addressee to cause a reaction, which in turn informs an action performed by the previous addressee, now turned addresser, upon the new addressee, which causes a reaction in the same way, and so on. Figure 3 shows the normal pattern of conversation between two people.

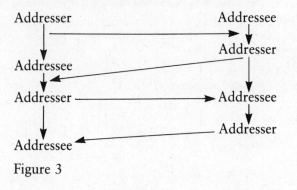

Figure 3

When involved in this reciprocal exchange, the participants are engaged in carrying out certain social actions. They perform these actions through language: they give orders, make promises, offer suggestions, tender apologies, lay bets, and so on. These are known as 'speech acts' (see Austin 1962, Searle 1969). Each utterance in a conversational interaction such as that outlined above can be seen as a speech act, a social action performed through language by the addresser, and intended to have some sort of effect upon the addressee.

▶ TASK 41

Decide what sort of speech act the addresser is probably trying to perform in each of the following utterances:

1 'I'll definitely have your essays marked by next Tuesday. You can have them back then.'
2 'Stop talking and sit down right now.'
3 'If only I had worked harder when I was on the course. If I hadn't been so lazy.'
4 'If you ever do that again, I'll send you to the headmaster with no excuses.'
5 'Please forgive me. I really am sorry, and I can assure you that it won't happen again.'
6 'You could try working in pairs rather than as a group now. That might give you more practice.'

a. making a promise   d. making a threat
b. giving an order   e. offering a suggestion
c. making an apology   f. making a wish

One interesting area of speech act theory is the differentiation between the addresser's intention and the addressee's interpretation. The addresser has an intention, a purpose, in performing any speech act. This is known as the 'illocutionary force' of the act, what the speaker intends the act to achieve.

The actual effect of the act is known as its 'perlocutionary effect', the reaction of the hearer to what the speaker says. In the same way that action does not always achieve the desired reaction, the addresser's intention in performing any speech act does not always match the addressee's interpretation of it.

▶ TASK 42

Study this short exchange:

Teacher: 'What are you laughing at, boy?'
Student: 'I'm laughing at this man I can see out of the window . . .'
Teacher: 'That's not what I meant!'

What *did* the teacher mean? What was the illocutionary force of his first utterance? But how did the student interpret it? What was its perlocutionary effect? What could the teacher have done/do now to ensure a match between his intentions and the student's interpretation of them? What, if anything, could the student have done/do now to ensure such a match?

4.5 Pedagogic interaction

The learning event describes the context for pedagogic interaction, the interaction of teaching and learning. This too, like verbal interaction, is a continuous, ever-changing process, and the factors of context shift from minute to minute.

The teacher acts upon the learners to cause a reaction. This reaction informs some action performed by the learners: a response to a question, an item executed in a drill, a word pronounced or spelt, a sentence written. The teacher studies this action, and perceives in it the reaction to her own original action. She in turn reacts and builds this into her subsequent action on the class, and so on. This is illustrated in Figure 4.

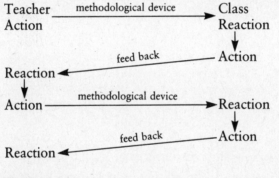

Figure 4

This should be the normal pattern of teaching and learning in a language class. The teacher should constantly monitor the students' reactions, and take account of these reactions at every stage of the lesson. This is the only check that the teacher has on learning.

The learning event parallels the speech event. Pedagogic interaction parallels verbal interaction. Teaching acts can parallel speech acts. For every activity the teacher employs, every drill, exercise, presentation, can be seen as a teaching act, a pedagogic action performed through methodological devices by the teacher, and intended to have a definite effect on the learner.

▶ TASK 43

Decide what sort of teaching act the teacher is probably trying to perform in employing each of the following activities. For example, number 1 is (a).

a. Providing opportunity for listening practice.
b. Providing practice in reading for gist.
c. Clarifying usage of specific grammar points.
d. Providing practice in pronunciation and intonation.
e. Checking how well a particular item has been mastered.
f. Providing new vocabulary items.

1 Teacher reads aloud while learners listen.
2 Learners have to draw pictures of main events in a narrative reading test.
3 Learners have to do a short blank-filling test on different tenses of the verbs *be/have/go*.
4 Learners are given a box of objects to each group, and a bilingual dictionary to find the names of the objects.
5 Learners read short passages aloud from textbooks.
6 Teacher lectures on the use of the definite article.

Each teaching act can be seen as having its own 'teaching force', what the teacher intends the act to achieve. The actual effect of the act can be seen as its 'learning effect', the reaction of the learner to what is being taught. Again, in actual practice, teacher intention does not always match learner interpretation, although communication cannot effectively take place unless it does so.

▶ TASK 44

Consider the following activities in their lesson context:

1 Teacher asks class to write adjectives on to sticky labels (as in the lesson described in 1.4).
2 Teacher gives class a short lyric poem to interpret (Task 40 above).
3 Teacher asks class to work in pairs on some pictures of Present Perfect tense activities (Task 2 above).

In each case, what was the teaching force of each activity? How did the learners interpret each activity? What was its learning effect? In each case, what could the teacher have done to ensure a match between the teaching force and the learning effect of the particular activity? What, if anything, could the learners have done to ensure such a match?

If the teacher is to achieve his objectives, then the learners must be able to perceive his intentions. If the intentions are unclear, or subject to misinterpretation, then the learners are unlikely to learn what the teacher wants them to learn. Both teacher and learners have to work at making the intentions clear, at securing a match between teacher intention and learner interpretation.

Describing

The first section of this book attempted to sort out and to define the various ideas and concepts involved in classroom interaction. This section examines these ideas and concepts more closely, and shows how they are made operational in the classroom context. From defining the different aspects of classroom interaction, we now move on to describing them.

5 Describing classroom language

In Unit 3 the notion of looking at classroom language to find out what is going on in a classroom was discussed. Language, after all, is highly observable and open to examination and description. Descriptions of classroom language can be undertaken for different purposes, and in different ways depending on these purposes.

5.1 To find out about language: Sinclair and Coulthard

As noted in 3.1 above, Sinclair and Coulthard (1975) used classroom verbal interaction as their data for research into discourse analysis. Classroom language, they felt, provided a relatively simple and more structured type of discourse than normal everyday conversation.

In their scheme for describing classroom data, the smallest unit of description is what they call *an act*. Here is a piece of classroom interaction described in terms of these acts.

 TASK 45

Study this piece of interaction and the 'acts' which describe each utterance. Can you give a definition for each of the eleven 'acts' used here on the basis of the sort of utterance it is applied to? For example:

metastatement = statement about the structure of the lesson.

Now try to do the same for the others:

marker	*nomination*
comment	*reply*
starter	*elicitation*
directive	*accept*
check	*prompt*

T: Well	*marker*
Today I thought we'd do three quizzes.	*metastatement*
We won't take the whole lesson to do	
a quiz because I want to talk to you	*comment*
some of the time.	
The first quiz is this. Can you fill	*starter*
in this sentence.	*starter*
See if you can do it in your books.	*directive*

	Finished Joan?	*check/nomination*
	And Miri?	*nomination*
St:	Yes	*reply*
T:	Finished?	*check*
Sts:	Yes	*reply*
T:	Right	*marker*
	Now	*marker*
	What are the letters that are missing?	*elicitation*
St:	e	*reply*
T:	Yes	*accept*
St:	a	*reply*
T:	a	*accept*
St:	a	*reply*
T:	Yes	*accept*
St:	o	*reply*
T:	And?	*prompt*
St:	e	*reply*
T:	And?	*prompt*
St:	u	*reply*
T:	u. Yes	*accept*
T:	Those letters have special names.	*starter*
	Do you know what it is?	*elicitation*

(Sinclair and Coulthard 1975: 63–4)

In the complete system devised by Sinclair and Coulthard, there are twenty-one acts altogether. Here is a list of them, with an explanation or examples given for each one. You can check your answers to Task 45 against this list, and see how well your definitions match the definitions or further examples given here.

Acts

Marker:	'well', 'right', 'OK', 'now'
Starter:	directing attention to a specific area
Elicitation:	question demanding linguistic response
Check:	'Finished?', 'Ready?', 'Any problems?'
Directive:	requesting a non-linguistic response
Informative:	providing information
Prompt:	'Have a guess', 'Come on, quickly'
Clue:	additional information to help student respond
Cue:	'Hands up', 'Don't call out'
Bid:	'Sir!', 'Miss!'
Nomination:	names of pupils, 'Who hasn't answered yet?'
Acknowledge:	'Yes', 'Mmm', 'OK'
Reply:	linguistic response to elicitation

React: non-linguistic response to directive
Comment: additional information, expanding, exemplifying
Accept: 'Yes', 'No', 'Good', 'Fine'
Evaluate: 'Good', 'Interesting', 'Fine'
Metastatement: helping pupils see the purpose and structure of the lesson
Conclusion: summarizing what has preceded
Loop: 'Pardon', 'Again', 'What did you say?'
Aside: 'Where's the chalk?', 'It's freezing in here'

► **TASK 46**

Now here is a continuation of the classroom verbal interaction given above. See if you can mark each act with its appropriate category from the list above:

		Act
T:	What is one name we give to those letters?	1
	Paul	2
Paul:	Er, vowels.	3
T:	They're vowels, aren't they?	4
T:	Do you think you could say that sentence without having the vowels in it?	5
	You knew what the vowels were because you'd heard 'the cat sat on the mat'.	6
	I tricked, I cheated by changing the last word.	7
	Could you say it without the vowel sounds?	8
Sts:	No (various noises)	9
T:	It's jolly hard isn't it. Ever so hard.	10
	Can you think why I changed 'mat' to 'rug'?	11
Sts:	Because, er	12
T:	Peter	13
Peter:	Mat's got two vowels in it.	14
T:	Which are they?	15
	What are they?	16
Peter:	'a' and 't'	17
T:	Is 't' a vowel?	18
S:	No	19
T:	No	20

► **TASK 47**

Sinclair and Coulthard did this work on classroom language for purely linguistic purposes, to find out more about the structure of spoken discourse. Do you think this sort of analysis of classroom language has anything to offer the teacher? Does it have anything to say about the sort of teaching and learning going on in a classroom? If so, what precisely can it do to help the teacher, do you think?

5.2 To find out about teaching and learning: BIAS

Descriptive frameworks in the Interaction Analysis tradition (see 3.1 and 3.2) aim to analyse classroom verbal interaction in order to find out something about the sort of teaching and learning going on. One fairly simple system in this tradition is Brown's Interaction Analysis System (BIAS) (Brown 1975). It is not intended specifically for the language classroom, but can usefully be applied to it.

Here are the basic categories of description in BIAS:

TL: *Teacher lectures*, describes, explains, narrates, directs.

TQ: *Teacher questions*, about content or procedure, which pupils are intended to answer.

TR: *Teacher responds*, accepts feelings of the class; describes past and future feelings in a non-threatening way; praises, encourages, jokes with pupils; accepts or uses pupils' ideas; builds upon pupil responses; uses mild criticism such as 'no, not quite'.

PR: *Pupils respond* directly and predictably to teacher questions and directions.

PV: *Pupils volunteer* information, comments, or questions.

S: *Silence*. Pauses, short periods of silence.

X: *Unclassifiable*. Confusion in which communications cannot be understood; unusual activities such as reprimanding or criticizing pupils; demonstrating without accompanying teacher or pupil talk; short spates of blackboard work without accompanying teacher or pupil talk.

These are essentially a simplification and reduction of Flanders' original ten categories (see 3.1).

 TASK 48

Can you match up any of Sinclair and Coulthard's categories with the BIAS categories TL, TQ, TR, PR, PV, S, and X?

Try to code the pieces of classroom verbal interaction given in Tasks 45 and 46 according to the BIAS categories rather than the Sinclair and Coulthard ones. For example:

T: Well   TL
       Today I thought we'd do three quizzes. We won't take
       the whole lesson to do a quiz because I want to talk

	to you some of the time. The first quiz is this.	
	Can you fill in this sentence?	
	See if you can do it in your books.	
	Finished Joan?	TQ
	And Miri?	
Miri:	Yes	PR
T:	Finished?	TQ

Now you continue with the rest of the interaction, in the same way.

In order to implement the BIAS System, a time-line display sheet is used and marked every three seconds for the duration of the observation. Figure 5 (from Brown 1975) shows an example of a time-line display sheet filled in for the first minute or so of a lesson:

TL = Teacher describes, explains, narrates, directs

TQ = Teacher questions

TR = Teacher responds to pupil's response

PR = Pupil responds to teacher's questions

PV = Pupil volunteers information, comments or questions

S = Silence

X = Unclassifiable

TL	/		/	/	/															
TQ						/			/		/		/							
TR							/	/				/						/	/	
PR		/				/					/			/	/					
PV																/				
S									/											
X	/																	/		

Figure 5

For ease of reference, a summary of the main categories is given at the head of the sheet. The observer records the appropriate category in each column every three seconds. Sometimes category X, the unclassifiable, has to be elaborated in order to clarify what is happening, for example *B = blackboard work, R = reprimanding students*.

Once a whole lesson has been coded in this way, percentages can be calculated for each of the categories noted, and a picture of the lesson built up. This picture can usefully be in the form of distribution tables or histograms. Two examples of these, taken from Brown (1975), are shown in Figure 6.

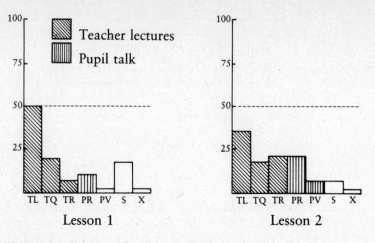

Figure 6

The pictures obtained of these two lessons show the percentages of each lesson taken up by the different categories, and the ratios of the different categories to each other in the lesson. This information is to be seen in the context of the type of lesson being taught, and in relation to its general aims and purposes.

▶ **TASK 49**

Looking at the two diagrams in Figure 6, what type of lesson do you think each represents? What kind of general lesson aim would best match each of these lesson profiles? Justify your answers.

Supposing the general aim of both lessons had been student practice in oral communication, which of the two lessons would you judge to have been the more successful? And why?

There is no such thing as a good or bad lesson pattern in itself; only a good or bad pattern in relation to the purpose of the lesson. A high percentage of TL might be undesirable in an oral practice lesson, but not, for example, in a listening comprehension lesson.

▶ **TASK 50**

Draw the type of histogram (using Figure 7 as a basis) that you would expect to get from

a. a reading comprehension lesson for an upper-secondary school class;
b. the presentation of a new structure to a beginners' class.

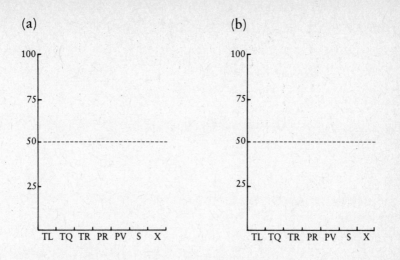

Figure 7

The time-line displays themselves provide interesting information about what goes on in a lesson. They demonstrate patterns and problems even before they are turned into tables of percentages and ratios. Figure 8, for example (from Brown 1975), shows a language drill going smoothly.

TL		/	/											
TQ				/		/		/		/				
TR														
PR					/		/		/		/			
PV														
S														
X	/													

Figure 8

But in the next example (Figure 9) there is a problem. The teacher gets no answer to his question, and provides the answer himself. The pupils keep quiet, and the teacher goes on answering his own questions.

TL			/	/		/	/									
TQ	/	/			/			/								
TR																
PR																
PV																
S			/			/			/							
X																

Figure 9

▶ TASK 51

Can you say what is going on in these lessons by looking at the patterns on the time-line displays? Give a short description of what is happening in Figure 10.

TL											/	/				
TQ	/	/	/		/	/		/								
TR																
PR																
PV																
S				/		/		/								
X																

Figure 10

And in Figure 11:

TL	/	/	/				/	/								
TQ				/				/								
TR					/											
PR				/				/								
PV																
S																
X																

Figure 11

5.3 To find out about the language classroom: Bowers

Bowers' categories of verbal behaviour in the language classroom (see 3.3) are directly derived from foreign-language classroom data. In order to implement this system of description, every utterance in a lesson has to be coded according to the relevant category, and a further note made as to whether it occurs in the mother tongue (MT) or target language (TL).

Here is a short sample of a transcript coded according to Bowers' categories:

T:	Yes. Right. The homework was well done.	*evaluating (TL)*
	Now put it away. Put it away. We'll start	*organizing (TL)*
	something else.	
St:	S'il vous plaît, Monsieur. S'il vous plaît. Vous	*eliciting (MT)*
	n'avez pas donné la réponse à 10c.	
T:	10c. 10c. You're right. Sorry. Small horse.	*responding (TL)*
	The answer is small horse. Now, all books	
	away. Look at me and listen carefully. The	*organizing (TL)*
	market. To the market. I went to the market.	*presenting (TL)*
	OK? Now after me – the market.	*eliciting (TL)*
Sts:	The market	*responding (TL)*
T:	To the market	*eliciting (TL)*
Sts:	To the market	*responding (TL)*
T:	Again. To the market. To the market.	*eliciting (TL)*
Sts:	To the market.	*responding (TL)*
T:	That's better.	*evaluating (TL)*
	I went to the market.	*eliciting (TL)*
Sts:	I went to the market.	*responding (TL)*
Sts:	I went to the market.	*responding (TL)*

There are five categories of verbal behaviour used in this short excerpt from a language lesson: *evaluating, organizing, eliciting, responding, presenting*. The other two categories in Bowers' system (see 3.3 above for complete system) are:

sociating: any act not contributing directly to the teaching/learning task, but rather to the establishment or maintenance of interpersonal relationships.

directing: any act encouraging non-verbal activity as an integral part of the teaching/learning task.

These categories are used to describe 'moves', the smallest unit of description in Bowers' system.

▶   TASK 52

Try to code the following short classroom exchanges according to
Bowers' system. Break each exchange down into moves first of all.
Then give the relevant category for each move. Finally, note (MT)
for the use of the mother tongue, or (TL) for the use of the target
language.

Moves

1 T: Now into pairs. Get into pairs with your
           neighbours. You're going to practise your
           dialogue together. In twos. What's wrong?
   St: Olamaz hocam.
   T: Neden, çoçuk?
   St: Ben tek başima. Komşum yok.
   T: Join this pair, Ali. You join this pair. You
           take turns at the dialogue between the three
           of you. First you two, then you two. Tamam
           mi?
   Sts: Tamam, hocam.

2 T: Well, you're all looking very cheerful today.
           Good weekend. Hm? Good weekend.
           Right, we'll start with a bit of revision.
           Juan, can you remember what we did on
           Friday? No? Maria, what about you?
   Maria: The Present Perfect.
   T: Good. Yes, the Present Perfect. Good.
           But the Present Perfect in relation to what . . .
           to what in particular? No? What two . . .
           which two prepositions? Which two little
           words?
   St: Since
   T: Since. Good. Yes. And? Since and . . .?
   St: For
   T: Yes. Very good. Since and for.

3 T: Bien. Très bien. Encore une fois.
           The book is on the table.
   Sts: The book is on the table.
   T: Un peu plus vite. Répétez.
           The book is on the table.

When an entire lesson has been coded in this way, percentages can be
calculated for each of the categories noted, and for use of mother tongue as
opposed to target language. In this way, a picture of the lesson can be built
up. A convenient way of doing this is in the form of histograms and
distribution tables, as with the BIAS examples in 5.2 above. But another
useful device for displaying information of this sort is in the form of a pie
chart. Figures 12 and 13, for example, show two pie charts drawn up from

data provided by coding lessons according to Bowers' system. The first is of a lesson comprising presentation of a new structure to the class, followed by some controlled drills.

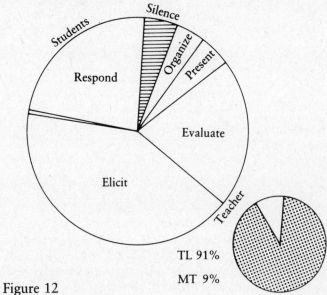

TL 91%

MT 9%

Figure 12

The second is of a lesson based on a translation exercise from a course book. Note the differences between the two lesson patterns.

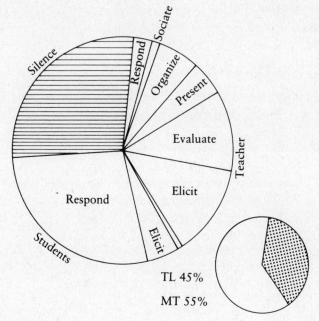

TL 45%

MT 55%

Figure 13

▶ **TASK 53**

Here are some data from a lesson coded according to Bowers'
system. Construct a pie chart to illustrate the following data:

MT: 0%	*responding*: 40%
TL: 100%	*sociating*: 5%
	organizing: 10%
	directing: 0%
	presenting: 10%
	evaluating: 5%
	eliciting: 30%

What sort of lesson do you think this might be? Give evidence for
your ideas.

5.4 To tell teachers what to do: Willis

The various systems and categories outlined above are all derived from
actual classroom data, and are all intended to act as frameworks of
description for what goes on, in verbal terms, in any lesson. They cannot be
used to judge the success of a lesson, or to prescribe what should go on in a
lesson, unless seen in conjunction with other factors, such as the general
purpose or content of the lesson in question.

They are not, however, to be seen as wholly objective instruments of
description. They are all subjective to the extent that they are based on
particular assumptions and preconceptions about the classroom. Sinclair
and Coulthard acknowledge that their system derives from data taken from
teacher-centred classrooms, for example.

▶ **TASK 54**

Look again at some of the systems of description outlined above:
– Sinclair and Coulthard's acts
– BIAS
– Bowers' moves
– FLINT categories (in 3.2).

Can you say anything about the assumptions that all or any of these
are based on with regard to:

1 The teacher's role in the classroom:
   – Is he/she the central focus?
   – Is he/she expected to be a stern, strict disciplinarian, or friendly
     and relaxed?
   – Does he/she do most of the talking?
     etc.

2 The students' roles in the classroom:
 - What is their main contribution to the verbal interaction?
 - Are they expected to instigate much interaction?
 - Who are they expected to communicate with most of the time?
   etc.

3 The pattern of teaching that goes on in the classroom:
 - Is it student-centred or teacher-centred?
 - Is the non-verbal an important element in teaching?
 - Is learning as important as teaching?
   etc.

Thus, although such schemes are not overtly prescriptive, in that they do not tell teachers directly what they are to do, they are still based on assumptions and expectations of what should be going on in the classroom. When these assumptions and expectations are made overt, we move from description to prescription, telling the teacher what to do.

Probably the best-known prescriptive approach to classroom language is Willis's *Teaching English Through English* (Willis 1981). In this scheme, classroom language is divided into two main categories:

1 language for social, personal, and organizational uses;
2 language for instructional uses.

The teacher is provided with the English to use in a variety of situations under each main heading.

These categories correspond closely to the purposes and content of classroom verbal communication outlined in Section One. Here are some examples of Willis's sub-categories included under 'social, personal, and organizational uses':

Beginning the lesson: greetings; informal conversation.

Physical conditions: comments on heat, light, noise, etc.

Using visual aids: organizing and indicating them.

Dividing the class up: managing choral, team, group, pair, and individual work.

► TASK 55

Using your work on Tasks 14 and 16 in Section One, try to predict what some of the other sub-categories under this 'social, personal and organizational' heading might be. Continue the list from the examples given above, with explanation and further detail, as necessary.

If you can obtain a copy of Willis's book, match your completed list with the contents of Part 1 of the book.

Willis's second main category is 'for instructional uses', corresponding to pedagogic purposes for communicating outlined in 2.2 and 2.4 above. Willis couples this category with methodology, providing the teacher in Part 2 of her book with instructions on what to do to express certain teaching points in the classroom, and what to say while doing it. Here are a few examples of her Part 2 unit headings and the instructional language accompanying them:

Dialogues
The people in this dialogue are going to . . .
I want you to listen again, and this time . . .

Teaching vocabulary
Who knows what this word means?
You all know the word . . .
Well, what's the opposite of it?

Listening skills
This is to give you practice in listening for . . .
Are you ready to listen and . . .
I'll start the tape.

Writing practice
Fill the blanks in these sentences and copy them neatly. Check your punctuation.

▶ **TASK 56**

Again, as in Task 55, try to extend this list of examples by predicting what some other unit headings for methodological areas might be, and by giving some examples of the sort of 'instructional language' that might be included under those headings.

Check your completed list against the contents of Part 2 of *Teaching English Through English*, if you can obtain a copy, and see how well the two match, if at all.

Teaching English Through English thus attempts to be a complete handbook for the English teacher, prescribing how to teach and what the teacher and the students should say in the course of the teaching and learning process.

▶ **TASK 57**

Willis's book is based on several assumptions. The first concerns the use of the target language in the classroom, and gives the book its name. What assumption is this? Do you think it is a fair assumption to make, or do you disagree with it?

Can you see any problems if teachers all over the world act on this assumption, and adopt the language promoted in the book? The results of your work on Task 55 might help you answer this question.

The second assumption concerns classroom methodology, the use of specified activities and techniques to achieve certain teaching objectives in the classroom. What assumption is this? Do you think it is a fair assumption to make, or do you disagree with it?

Can you see any problems if teachers all over the world act on this assumption, and adopt the methodology promoted in Part 2 of *Teaching English Through English*? The results of your work on Task 56 might help you answer this question.

Finally, are there any other important assumptions that you think underlie Willis's book? What are they? The results of your work on Task 54 might help you here.

Any prescriptive scheme for classroom language or methodology must suffer from the same type of drawbacks as any descriptive scheme: namely, that what is applicable in one context will not necessarily be appropriate in another.

6 Describing classroom methodology

6.1 Observation instruments

Language is observable. What is said in the classroom, by teacher or student, can be recorded and written down. These authentic data can be examined, categorized, analysed, by any of the means already described.

On the same principle, observation instruments have been devised for the observables of the classroom pedagogic interaction, the teaching and learning that goes on in the classroom. This involves focusing on various aspects of classroom methodology, the strategies, activities, and techniques that the teachers employ to communicate their teaching point.

In 3.4 above, three such instruments were touched on: COLT, TALOS, and that devised by Mitchell and Parkinson. The various categories employed by each of these instruments under the headings of *topic* or *content* and *language activity* were considered. There are, of course, other aspects of classroom methodology worth noting besides these two. There is the particular language skill (or mixture of skills) being emphasized in any activity; there is the way the class is organized for the activity, in groups, pairs, on individual tasks, or as a whole; there is the sort of materials being used; and there are the different roles adopted by teacher and by learners in the particular activity in question.

6.2 Mitchell and Parkinson

The Mitchell and Parkinson instrument for the analysis of strategies of foreign-language teaching in Scottish secondary schools is laid out in full in Table 1. To the basic dimensions of *topic* and *activity* it adds three other dimensions concerned with the role played by the teacher, the activity focus of the students, and the general organization of the class.

▶ TASK 58

Look at the Teacher-Mode categories in the Mitchell and Parkinson instrument. Try to give an example of a classroom activity for each category, for example:

T. not involved – class doing written test.

Table 1: The Mitchell and Parkinson instrument for the analysis of strategies of foreign-language teaching

TOPIC	LANGUAGE ACTIVITY	T-MODE	P-MODE	CLASS ORGANIZATION
Civilization	Interpretation	Not involved	± Listening	Whole class
General linguistic notions	LI	Instructing	± Speaking	Pupil demonstration
Language points (course)	Real FL	Interacting	± Doing	Co-operative, same task
Language points (other)	Transposition	Watching/helping	± Reading	Co-operative, different task
Situation (course)	Presentation	Participating	± Writing	Individual, same task
Real life	Drill/exercise	Working with group	± Looking	Individual, different task
Fragmented/noncontextualized	Compound	Working with individual		
Pupil performance				Co-operative and individual
Routine procedures				
Other				

Now look at the *Class organization* categories. Try to give an example of a classroom activity for each of these, for example:

Whole class – repetition drill *or* listening comprehension.

Now look at the Pupil-Mode categories. Why do you think there is a + and a – sign in front of each one? Can you give the reason? Can you give any examples of a classroom activity which would be + Listening – Speaking – Doing + Reading + Writing – Looking?

▶ **TASK 59**

Looking at the whole Mitchell and Parkinson system, in Table 1, could you implement it in the same way as the systems to describe verbal interaction were implemented?

Would you code each utterance, as with Bowers' system? Or would you make a coding every three seconds, as with BIAS? If these types of implementation are not feasible, what would you suggest instead?

Mitchell and Parkinson suggest that the various categories be applied to *segments* of a lesson, units longer than a single utterance, or even an exchange of the question-and-answer type, but shorter than an entire lesson. These segments exemplify continuous patterns of behaviour over a period of time, and correspond in many ways to teachers' own ideas about the sub-divisions of their lessons.

Segments can often be recognized by the teacher's summing up of an activity just completed, and launching of a new activity with words like 'right', 'now', 'OK', and so on. Often a teacher will describe what is going to happen next: 'Now, you are going to hear a dialogue.' Or she will simply issue a direction to the pupils: 'Now, listen and repeat.'

These segments correspond to a unit of description in the Sinclair and Coulthard scheme (see 5.1) known as a 'transaction'. Any lesson, in their terms, comprises one or more transactions, and the boundaries of any transaction are clearly marked by phrases such as 'now', 'well', 'right then', and so on, which act as 'framing' devices for the transaction in question.

Mitchell and Parkinson say that these segments correspond to 'patterns of expectation' in the pupils' minds. This means that pupils and teacher share an understanding of what is going on at any given time. If the teacher says: 'Write down what I say', the class will understand a dictation exercise, and continue writing down what the teacher says until a new order is given to break that pattern. With the breaking of the pattern comes the end of that particular segment of the lesson, and the beginning of a new one.

► TASK 60

Can you identify the *segments* in the following piece of classroom transcript (from the British Council video tape *Teaching and Learning in Focus*, 1985)? How many are there? What words are used to introduce each segment?

Teacher: Right hello everybody.
Students: Hello.

T: Right – um – I've brought an old friend to see you again today. Can you remember who he is?
SS: Er – yes – yes.
T: What's his name? Can you remember his name?
SS: Dr Newton – Dr Newton – Dr Newton.
T: His name is Dr Newton OK. Right what does he do? What's his job? Any idea what his job is?
SS: He's a doctor – doctor.
T: He's a doctor, yes, he's a doctor. Why do we go – why do we go – to the doctor?
S: It's because – because we are . . .
T: Got a – what have I got. Can't talk very well. What's the matter? What's the matter? Uh let's have a look. What's he got? What's he got? Um – yes, he's got a bad cold. He's got a bad cold.

(**Caption:** Eunice [the teacher] practises 'sore throat and cough' in same way.)

Nelson: He's got a headache.
T: Perfect – right, again.
Nelson: He's got a headache.
T: A headache, he's got a headache, everybody.
SS: He's got a headache.
T: He's got a headache.
SS: He's got a headache.
T: He's got a headache. Oh dear dear! Let's put him there shall we. What's the matter with him?
SS: He's got – he's got – he's got – flu – flu – sore throat—sore – sore throat.
T: He's got a –.
SS: Sore throat.
T: Sore throat. He's got a sore throat. Everybody.
SS: He's got a sore throat.
T: He's got a sore throat.
SS: He's got a sore throat.
T: What's the matter with him?
SS: He's got a bad cold – bad cold.
T: What's the matter with him?
SS: He's got a cough.
T: He's got a cough, yes. Let's have a look at this one.

(**Caption:** After more practice Eunice gives key questions for guided listening.)

T: Can you read the questions? No no, just read them yourself. Right three questions, we're going to listen to the tape and try to find the answers to the questions. Right just listen. Any problems with questions, anybody doesn't understand . . .?

Cassette: Now Mr Wilson, what's the matter with you? I've got a bad cold, doctor. Have you got a cough? No I haven't got a cough, but I've got a sore throat. . . .

Cassette: I see. Mr Wilson. Yes. Come and see me again next week please. OK. Goodbye doctor. Goodbye.

T: Right. Have a look at the questions, and let's see if we've got the answers. How many people are there? Just a shout.

SS: Two

T: Two, everybody agrees? Just two.

SS: Yes.

T: Right. Yes, just two. Where are they?

SS: In the – office.

T: Where? In the . . . whose office?

SS: Er – a doctor's – a doctor's office – office doctor.

T: Doctor office – doctor.

SS: Doctor's office.

T: Fine right. The doctor's office. What do we call a doctor's office in English? Go on, go on, Louisa fine, say it.

Louisa: Consult – consultation.

T: It's a consultation that they are going to give, it's a very good try, a good try. We call it a surgery, a surgery. The office is called a surgery. All right, fine OK. Right. Some more questions for you. Read them. OK let's just go through them together. Make sure you understand. The patient's name is Mr Wilson. He's got a bad cold and a cough. . . .

T: What I want you to do is to put numbers on a piece of paper 1–8 all right? Listen to the tape and write if the statement is true or if the statement is false. OK? Any problems with the questions? No problems. Great.

Using the Mitchell and Parkinson categories, the first segment identified in the transcript above can be described as follows:

Segment 1
topic:	language point (course)
activity:	drill
T-Mode:	instructing
P-Mode:	+ looking + speaking + listening
class organization:	whole class

TASK 61

Can you describe the other segments you identified from the transcript in the same way?

6.3 COLT: Communicative Orientation of Language Teaching

COLT, the Content and Activity sections of which are outlined in 3.4 above, takes a very similar approach to what is being observed in the classroom. With this instrument, the observer concentrates on each activity and describes it in his or her own terms – listening comprehension exercise with pre-set questions; introduction of new vocabulary, or whatever. The observer also notes the starting time of each activity in the classroom.

Each activity is then categorized according to *content* (see 3.4 above); *student modality* (Listening, Speaking, Reading, Writing or Other); *participant organization* (Class, Group, Individual or Combination of any of those); and *materials*. The latter category covers *type* of material: textbook, audio, visual; pedagogic (i.e. specially devised for teaching purposes), semi-pedagogic or non-pedagogic; and *use* of material: highly controlled, semi-controlled, minimally controlled.

▶ TASK 62

Look again at the transcript of part of a lesson in Task 60 above. If you were coding this lesson according to the COLT instrument,

a. how would you describe each of the activities in the lesson?
b. what would you say about the material used for each activity?

6.4 TALOS: Target Language Observation Scheme

A far more ambitious and extensive instrument than either of the above is TALOS, again first introduced in 3.4 above. This contains both a high-inference section, demanding subjective impressions of various aspects of a lesson, and a low-inference section, for on-the-spot coding of classroom observables. This coding takes place for periods of thirty seconds in duration, followed by a ninety-second period when no coding takes place, and the observer is free to look around the class in order to obtain more subjective, global impressions of what is going on. The two types of information are seen as being of equal value.

Table 2: The Target Language Observation Scheme (TALOS): Low-inference section

	WHO – TEACHER																													
Observation Unit	**To whom**				**What – Type of activity Formal–Functional Focus**							**Content Focus**							**Skill Focus**				**Teaching Medium**							
	Large	Small	Individual	Other	drill	dialogue	frame	spelling	translation	paraphrasing	free communication	**Linguistic**				**Substan-tive**		integrated subject matter	listen	speak	read	write	text	A.V.	authentic materials	draw	poem	song	game	role playing
												sound	word	phrase	discourse	grammar	culture													
1 b																														
c																														
2 b																														
c																														
3 b																														
c																														
4 b																														
c																														
5 b																														
c																														
6 b																														
c																														
7 b																														
c																														
8 b																														
c																														
9 b																														
c																														
10 b																														
c																														

WHO – TEACHER (cont'd)															WHO – STUDENT																
Teaching Act													L Use		To whom					What – Type of utterance							Type of question				L Use	
drill	narrate	explain	discuss	compare	answer	meta-comments & questions	cognitive questions	low level questions	correct	reinforce	routine	discipline	L 1	L 2	large	small	peer	teacher	other	sound	word	sentence fragment	sentence	extended discourse	non verbal	no response	meta-comments & questions	cognitive Q	low Q	routine Q	L 1	L 2

Table 2 presents the low-inference section of TALOS. The categories contained in it are glossed by Ullman and Geva (1984) as follows.

1 'Teacher' section

a. *To whom* reflects who is being addressed by the teacher on a continuum from large group to individuals.

b. *What type of activity* refers to classroom activities initiated by the teacher to achieve pedagogical goals. These activities are arranged on a continuum from formal to functional, beginning at the formal end with 'drill' and ending with the most open-ended activity 'free communication'.

c. *Content focus* is subdivided into linguistic content and substantive content. By linguistic content we refer to the emphasis on the formal properties of the L2, namely sound, word, phrase or discourse. By substantive content we refer to overt formal grammar teaching, the explicit development of cultural information during the lesson and the introduction and integration of other subject matter into the second-language program.

d. *Skill focus* describes the listening, speaking, reading, and writing skills practised in each lesson segment. The skill focus category makes clear the skill-building intent and purpose of each activity and each teaching act undertaken by the teacher.

e. *Teaching medium* refers to those heuristic devices which the teacher uses in order to develop the formal or functional focus of the lesson, the substantive content in the lesson or the skill-building intent of the activity.

f. *Teaching act* refers to pedagogical verbal strategies used by the teacher to enhance learning in the students, such as teaching acts that are directly related to the lesson at hand, e.g., 'explain' and 'correct', as well as teaching acts which relate to classroom management, e.g. 'routine' and 'discipline'.

g. *Language use* relates to the crosslingual-intralingual continuum and describes the language used in the classroom by students and teachers. It provides information about the relative amount of L1 and L2 used, and in conjunction with other activities, it provides information about the circumstances under which each language is being used.

2 'Student' section

a. *What type of utterance* deals with the individual student responses to teacher-initiated prompts. The entries in this category may be either verbal or non-verbal. The verbal responses are arranged on an utterance-size continuum starting with a single sound and ending with extended discourse. A 'note response' entry is also included in this category.

b. *Type of question* describes student-initiated questions, e.g., cognitive questions and questions relating to classroom management and routines.

(From Ullman and Geva 1984)

▶ TASK 63

Try to code the following short excerpts from the lesson transcript in Task 60 according to these TALOS categories:

1 From **Nelson**:   *He's got a headache . . .*
   To **SS**:   *Sore throat.*

2 *From* **Cassette**: *Now, Mr Wilson . . .*
   To **Cassette**:   *Goodbye doctor. Goodbye.*

Observation instruments such as the three described above can be used to build up a comprehensive profile of the sort of teaching methodology practised in any classroom or set of classrooms. The data provided by such instruments can be useful to a variety of people for a variety of reasons.

▶ TASK 64

In what ways do you think the data provided by instruments such as those described above might be useful to:

1 teacher trainees
2 curriculum developers
3 textbook writers
4 inspectors of schools
5 the teacher(s) observed?

6.5 Teaching methodology: description

To be useful to the practising teacher, or teacher trainee, observation instruments do not have to be as comprehensive or as formal as those outlined above. Much can be learnt from applying a simple instrument aimed at raising awareness about, or focusing attention upon, specific areas of methodology. These may be areas of practice which require improvement. For example, error correction is an important part of any teacher's methodological practice, and one which is often neglected, or dealt with summarily on teacher-training courses. It is an area which could be focused on by using an observation instrument such as that in Table 3.

Method of correction	Type of error		
	Grammar	Vocabulary	Pronunciation
1 Teacher gives correct answer.			
2 Teacher asks other S – 'Is that right?' 'What's wrong?'			
3 Teacher says 'No/wrong.'			
4 Teacher says 'Again/repeat.'			
5 Teacher mentions term e.g. tense, third person, pronoun.			
6 Teacher repeats question with change of stress.			
7 Teacher repeats student's answer up to point of error.			
8 Teacher makes physical gesture to indicate error.			
9 Teacher does not correct.			

Table 3

▶ # TASK 65

Now apply the observation instrument above to the following short piece of classroom interaction (which is taken from the British Council video tape *Teaching and Learning in Focus*, 1985).

Teacher: OK Driss you are walking down the street with Mr Miftah. You are very good friends. OK? What, what do you say to Mr Miftah?

Driss: Um, er, could you passing me – er – one cigarette, please?

T: I don't think so. I don't think so. (+ gesture)

Driss: Do you think . . . I want a cigarette.

T: OK, you could say I want a cigarette and what would you say Mr Miftah?

Miftah: Of course. Here, here you are.

T: OK, so he gives you a cigarette Driss and now you want something else. So what, so what do you ask for now?

SS: Matches, matches.

S: Matches? Fire?

T: Yeah but you don't say matches or fire. (laugh). What do you ask him?

S: Er – can you please . . . er . . . give me fire?

T: Fire.

S: Give me

T: A light yes. We say 'a light' in English. So we'd say 'Can you please give me a light' or . . .

S: Have you got any matches?

T: Have you got any matches? OK.

What, precisely, do you think a teacher or student teacher can learn from being observed in this way?

Observation exercises of this type can also be used to clarify areas of difficulty in teacher-training work. For example, the concept of 'communicative' language teaching can be a difficult one to grasp, however much a trainer tries to explain it or give examples of it. Instances of real communication in the target language, and the opportunity to make them occur in the classroom, are not always easily recognizable. The teacher may be too busily occupied with executing the lesson plan, or may confuse communicative teaching with some other notion, such as direct method.

A simple observation exercise can be used to focus attention on instances of communicative teaching in a lesson. First, the teacher to be observed is asked to mark his or her lesson plan for any communicative elements in it. Then an observer identifies what he or she perceives as the communicative elements in the lesson, using a checksheet such as that shown in Table 4.

Description of communicative event	Stage of lesson at which it occurs	How many people involved	Planned or not
1 Excuses from latecomers.	Before lesson really started	T + 3 students	Not
2 Student didn't understand an example. Asked for explanation.	Presentation stage	T + 1 student	Not
3 Communication game: Find the Difference.	Free practice stage	All students in pairs	Yes
4			

Table 4

At the end of the lesson, the observer's list is matched with the teacher's lesson plan, along with the teacher's subjective impression of what unplanned communicative elements had arisen as the lesson developed. This exercise serves to focus attention on specific parts of the lesson, and any mismatch between the two views of what was communicative in the lesson can be fruitfully discussed.

▶ TASK 66

Devise an observation exercise, on the lines of the two examples given above for *error correction* and *communicative teaching*, to deal with one of the following situations:

1 Your colleagues say that they already use a lot of pair work in their lessons. You know that they do not. You want them to realize how little pair work and group work they actually do.

2 The teachers you work with have very little variation in their lessons – all drill-work, or all reading comprehension, and so on. You want to focus their attention on the lack of variety of activity in their lessons.

3 Some of your colleagues have difficulty in timing different activities in their lessons, with the result that they rarely manage to finish what they plan to do. You want to help them to see the importance of timing, and the way they themselves manage (or mismanage) time in their own lessons.

6.6 Teaching methodology: prescription

Observation instruments focus on what is actually happening in a class. They are essentially descriptive. But most teachers see methodology as being essentially prescriptive. They are more concerned with what they think they should be doing in a class, than with what is actually happening. And there are plenty of directives as to what they should be doing, how they should teach.

Teachers' notes accompanying the textbook in use tell the teacher what he or she should do. Lecturers at teacher training college gave the teacher trainee prescriptions for how to teach certain items and areas. Books like Willis's *Teaching English Through English* (see 5.4 above) are full of instructions on methodological procedures and routines. Schemes for teaching assessment and evaluation have their own in-built preconceptions of what is wanted, of what the manifestations of 'good' teaching are.

Table 5, for example, is part of an assessment form that is used to assess teachers in classrooms all over the world. It is the Check List for Practical Tests used in the examination for the Diploma For Overseas Teachers of English run by the Royal Society of Arts (reproduced here with permission).

PERSONAL QUALITIES	GRADE	COMMENTS
Personality–'Presence' general style		
Ability to establish rapport		
Voice–Audibility, ability to project		
PREPARATION	**GRADE**	**COMMENTS**
Lesson plan, balance and variety of activities, timing		
Clarity, limitation and specification of aim		
Suitability of materials and methods for level and type of class		
EXECUTION	**GRADE**	**COMMENTS**
Techniques of class management		
Progress through the lesson, changes in activity, pace, etc		
Presentation of materials: Meaningful, motivated, contextualized, appropriately staged		
Questioning: graded, directed appropriate		
Controlled practice: choral-individual		
Ability to foster genuine language use		
Awareness and correction of errors		
Use of blackboard or equivalent		

Table 5   *(continued overleaf)*

EXECUTION	GRADE	COMMENTS
Use of other aids		
Maintenance of interest		
Involvement and encouragement of learners		
Checking of learning		
Achievement of aims		
Ability to adapt and extemporize (if necessary)		
Understanding and handling of: Structure Lexis Phonology		
Handling of text, dialogue, etc., if presented		

 ## TASK 67

If you were a teacher about to undergo assessment on the basis of the form in Table 5,

1 What sort of classroom personality would you feel you had to project?
2 What sort of lesson plan would you feel obliged to prepare?
3 What sort of activities would you feel it necessary to include in your lesson?
4 How would you feel you had to behave during the course of the lesson?

Try writing a lesson plan (choose any level of class and any materials you wish) that you think would gain you a good pass or a distinction on the basis of this form.

Outline the sort of lesson, giving details of class level and materials used, that you think it might be best to avoid for the purposes of this assessment. It should be a well-taught lesson, but one which will not, by its very nature, attract such good marks on the basis of this assessment form.

The pressure to conform to externally set standards and prescribed categories like this leads to many teachers exhibiting what they consider to be the most desirable performance in the circumstances. Thus they may stick rigidly to approved lesson plans. They may go unthinkingly through classroom rituals. They may talk of 'the best method' and 'the new method' as if there were one solution to all problems of classroom teaching. They may adopt classroom personalities at direct variance with their own real-life personalities. And all in the name of 'good' teaching.

6.7 Teaching and learning: the student

In the classroom, what the teacher says and does is observable. What and how he or she teaches is observable too. What the students say and do is equally observable, though, by the very nature of the classroom situation, their saying and doing amount to a lot less than the teacher's. What the student learns is not open to observation in the same way.

Hence, in looking at the classroom, the focus tends to be on the teacher, because the teacher's activities can easily be seen. The emphasis is on teaching, and information about the learners is generally subordinate to this.

 TASK 68

Look at some of the observation instruments described on the previous pages. What sort of information about the student/learner does each instrument provide? What exactly does each instrument tell us about the student? Take, for example:

– FIAC in 3.1;
– Bowers' categories in 3.3;
– Mitchell and Parkinson's instrument in 6.2;
– TALOS in 6.4;
– RSA assessment checklist in 6.6.

Do any of these instruments provide information on the learning (or lack of it) going on in the lesson observed?

The main point of being in a classroom is for learning to take place. This is the aim of the classroom transaction, the learner's reception of the teaching message being every bit as important as the teacher's delivery of it. What goes on inside the learners is therefore crucial in any examination of teaching practice. Successful learning is the main criterion of teaching success.

► ## TASK 69

Clearly, what and how a learner learns in the classroom cannot be observed in quite the same way as what a learner says, or what and how a teacher teaches. Can you think of any way(s) of finding out about the learning that goes on in a classroom? How can the learner be 'looked at'?

Verbal communication is achieved by co-operative interaction (see 1.5 above). The speaker tries to make his intentions accessible and acceptable to the hearer. The hearer, for his part, tries to make sure he has understood the speaker's intentions correctly. Both parties are responsible for achieving the communication desired.

The situation is the same for teaching and learning in the classroom. Teacher and student are both responsible for the pedagogic communication that is achieved. The teacher uses methodology to put her point over. The student must try to interpret the methodology and get something out of the activities which the class is asked to engage in. In the same way as co-operative interaction achieves verbal communication, it is also necessary to achieve pedagogic communication.

► ## TASK 70

In 4.5 above, you looked at ways in which the teacher can encourage co-operative interaction in the classroom, by checking on what the students are getting out of the lesson, and on what they understand from the various activities they are asked to engage in. Can you think of any other devices a teacher can employ for this purpose?

A student comes out of a lesson saying, 'I didn't get anything out of that', or 'What was she driving at?' or, 'Why do you suppose he made us do that exercise?' Do you think the teacher is to be blamed, or does the student bear any responsibility for this reaction?

If the student is unclear about whether he has grasped a teaching point correctly, or whether he has learned what the teacher intended him to learn, what can he do to remedy the situation?

What can a teacher do to encourage students to take some responsibility for the reception of the teaching message in the classroom?

Learning, of course, goes on outside the classroom as well as inside it. There has been a great deal of research in recent years on the ways in which different students approach language learning in general. Here is a list of learning strategies derived from one such piece of research (Rubin and Thompson, 1982):

1 Find your own way.
2 Organize.
3 Be creative.
4 Make your own opportunities.
5 Learn to live with uncertainty.
6 Use mnemonics.
7 Make errors work.

8 Use your linguistic knowledge.
9 Let context help you.
10 Learn to make intelligent guesses.
11 Learn some lines as wholes.
12 Learn formalized routines.
13 Learn production techniques.
14 Use different styles of speech.

▶ TASK 71

Which of these strategies do you think would be useful for learners:

a. coping with formal teaching and learning inside the classroom;
b. working on their own outside the classroom;
c. both of the above situations.

Thinking back to your own language-learning experience, which, if any, of these strategies did you employ? Can you add any other strategies to the list from your own experience?

It is, of course, sometimes said that learning can take place without teaching, that teachers are not necessary to the learning process. Learners do, after all, learn languages from books, or pick languages up simply by being in environments where the languages are spoken.

By the same token, learning is often said to take place despite teaching, in that learners manage to learn a language even if they are exposed to extremely weak and ineffective teaching. But the very existence of such concepts as 'teach-yourself books' or 'self-taught language speakers' seems to imply that some sort of teaching accompanies all learning, albeit not always of the traditional teacher-in-a-classroom sort.

▶ TASK 72

How do you react to these statements?

1 Learning can take place without teaching.
2 Learning can take place despite teaching.
3 Teachers are not necessary for learning.

Do you agree, or disagree, with each of them? On what grounds?

7   Describing classroom affect

The way the teacher and students feel about each other, about themselves, and about what is going on in the classroom is another important area for examination. These affective factors contribute a great deal to the success, or lack of it, of the classroom interaction.

7.1   As an observer: one man's meat . . .

In 3.5 above, it was pointed out how difficult it is to analyse the affective factors operating in any classroom. Moskowitz's FLINT contains categories like:

>   Teacher smiles
>   Laughter
>   Praises or encourages
>   Jokes
>   Corrects without rejection.

The high-inference section of TALOS (see 6.4 above) contains categories under the 'Teacher' section like:

>   Humour
>   Enthusiasm.

The RSA assessment check-list (see 6.6) lists under 'Personal Qualities':

>   Ability to establish rapport
>   'Presence'.

▶   TASK 73

>   What are the assumptions behind these categories? What is the picture of the ideal teacher that they tend to establish and reinforce? In observation schemes like these what type of classroom atmosphere is presented as being most conducive to learning?

One man's meat is another man's poison. These observation schemes were drawn up by particular individuals in specific contexts. There are doubtless other individuals with whom, and other contexts in which, these assumptions do not hold. Learning can be effected with a joke, or with a reprimand. Praise can encourage, but criticism can provoke action too. A quiet, self-effacing teacher can put over her points as well as a teacher of 'presence'.

To describe classroom affect accurately, both positive and negative features must be accounted for. And a decision can be made only in subjective terms as to whether it is positive or negative affect that is being displayed. A laughing and joking class might be the ideal to some, but appear chaotic bedlam to others.

▶   TASK 74

If you were looking for signs of positive affect in a classroom, i.e. signs that the sort of atmosphere necessary for co-operative interaction between teacher and students existed, what would you look for in

the teacher's attitude and behaviour?
the students' attitudes and behaviour?
the general classroom atmosphere?

What by contrast would you read as being signs of negative affect on the part of teachers and students?

Some of the categories dealing with affect (from FLINT, TALOS, RSA) outlined above might give you some ideas for answering, or thinking about, these questions.

In the final analysis, accurate observation and description of the feelings experienced by the participants in any interaction situation are impossible. Only the interactants themselves can talk with any authority of the affective factors in the classroom situation.

7.2 As a teacher: 'humanistic' techniques

A trend has recently developed in methodological techniques and approaches which stresses the affective factors of the classroom situation. Where once methodology stressed the classroom transaction, it now concentrates on the *interaction* (see 2.3 above). This move from transaction to interaction necessarily brings in the human factor, in that it focuses not on the objective of teaching, but on the process of achieving that objective. Hence the concern for affect, and the various developments in this area that have come to be known collectively as 'humanistic' techniques.

The lesson scenario given in 1.4 is an example of this 'humanistic' teaching. The emphasis on relaxation, and the encouragement of group dynamics within the class, are hallmarks of the approach.

Moskowitz, designer of FLINT, is a prime mover in this trend. In her book, *Caring and Sharing in the Foreign Language Classroom*, she provides many examples of 'humanistic' exercises. Here is one of them, entitled 'The best product – me'.

Purposes:

Affective:

To get students to be introspective in a lighthearted way.

To call on students' creativity and imagination.

For fun.

Linguistic:

To practise the use of superlatives.

To practise the use of adjectives describing positive qualities.

To practise forming interrogative sentences.

Levels: All levels.

Size of groups: Six to eight or the total class.

Materials needed: A brochure or ad made by each student.

Procedures: In giving the assignment to the class, say something similar to this: 'Wherever we turn, we are surrounded by advertisements. Every few minutes television broadcasts commercials. Magazines and newspapers are filled with ads. And even driving in a car, the radio and billboards on the highway overwhelm us with advertising. All of the products, we are told, are the best on the market.

'Since we are so familiar with advertising, we are going to write some commercials. The product each of you will write about is very special and very rare. The product is *YOU*!

'Think about yourself and what makes you so unique. Then design an ad or a brochure selling your product to readers. You can use coloured paper on tag board. Magazine pictures, snapshots, sketches, and three-dimensional objects can be used for your commercial. Use the foreign language in writing your ad. Remember to rave about how great, how extraordinary, how remarkable your product is and what it can do for others.

'We will all get to see the ads or brochures you create, so use your imagination and remember how good your product is as you try to sell it.' (Encourage creativity and you will get it.)

When the ads are brought in, divide the students into groups of six to eight. Have each student pass his ad to the person on his right. Everyone will then read the ad to himself to get the flavour of it. Then, one at a time, the students will read the ad aloud and show it to the group. (This means no one is reading his own ad, so embarrassment will be reduced.)

Next the groups should volunteer to have two of their advertisements read to the entire class. The owners of the ads could now read them before the class. Then instruct the students to hang their ads on the wall, and let the class circulate around the room reading them. As they do so, have the students each compose five questions based on the ads they read, and select some to ask before their former groups or the total class. This will keep the class actively rather than passively involved with the ads. It is fun and humorous to see whether you can remember 'Who the product is' in this follow-up quiz activity.

An alternative to dividing the class in groups at first is to have the class seated in a circle, with each person passing his ad to the one on his right to be read aloud and shown to the class. The advertisements can still be posted around the room afterwards with the quiz following.

(Moskowitz 1978)

▶ TASK 75

What assumptions are made in this exercise about

1 the teacher who will use it;
2 the students who are expected to participate in it;
3 the sorts of resources available?

Give evidence from the exercise for your answers. Look at the Affective Purposes of the exercise stated at the beginning of it. Would you agree that all of these purposes are worthwhile ones to try to achieve in the course of a language lesson?

7.3 Counselling Language Learning

A complete 'humanistic' approach to language learning is Counselling Language Learning (CLL) (see Curran 1972). Here is a typical CLL classroom scenario:

The students, about twelve of them, are sitting in a circle. There is a small table in the centre of the circle with a tape-recorder and a microphone on it. One of the students begins a sentence in English: 'I went to the cinema . . .', falters, hesitates, and continues in Spanish, his native language. The teacher goes up behind him, whispers in his ear, and the student, clearly repeating what the teacher has said to him, comes out with: 'I went to the cinema to see "Rambo" on Saturday.' The teacher motions him to repeat this sentence and switches on the tape-recorder so that this repetition can be captured on tape. Immediately, another student in the circle responds with 'Was you enjoy it?' The teacher goes up to this student, whispers in his ear, and the student corrects himself with 'Did you enjoy it?' A further repetition of this corrected version is then recorded on tape.

The class continues like this for some minutes, students stumbling out their contributions to the conversation, the teacher playing a low-key, supportive role throughout. After some time, the teacher stops the conversation, and plays back the tape-recorded version. She then takes this version, one sentence at a time, and writes each sentence up on the board, drawing attention to points of grammar, spelling, and punctuation. The teacher uses this material as the basis of a grammar lesson, concentrating on those grammatical patterns which the students need to know well.

▶   TASK 76

How would you describe the teacher's role in CLL? In what way(s) does the CLL classroom experience differ from the traditional one for the learner?

Looking at the sort of transaction, the teaching and learning of language items, that goes on in a CLL lesson like this one, can you see any particular advantages or disadvantages in this approach?

7.4 Suggestopedia

Suggestopedic techniques also come under the heading of 'humanistic' approaches to language learning. The basic idea behind suggestopedia is to make the learner totally relaxed, open, and receptive to what he is learning (see Lozanov 1978). Any barriers built up by negative feelings or resentments are to be broken down before learning can take place.

Comfortable seating and pleasant classroom décor play a part in achieving these ends. Each student is given a foreign-language name, and a fictitious prestigious occupation at the outset of the course. The teacher maintains an air of benign authority throughout, exuding self-confidence and encouraging self-confidence in the students.

The material of authentic suggestopedic courses consists principally of dialogues. These are printed in a special way, with a native-language translation in a parallel column. There are set techniques for the handling of these dialogues in the classroom:

Step One
The teacher reads the text of the dialogue and the students follow in their books. The teacher answers any questions the students may have about the dialogue, and this question-and-answer session is conducted in the native language.

Step Two
The students put their books aside and sit back comfortably in their chairs as the teacher reads the dialogue again. This reading is done in a very particular, modulated way.

Step Three
A third reading by the teacher is accompanied by carefully chosen classical music. The students are still seated comfortably in their chairs, and do not refer to their books.

Step Four
Various kinds of exploitation of the dialogue. Oral and written exercises of the kind used by language teachers everywhere.

▶ TASK 77

Contrast Suggestopedia with Counselling Language Learning. What are the main differences between the two? What, if any, are the similarities? Consider as points of contrast

1 the role played by the teacher;
2 the roles played by the students;
3 the general classroom atmosphere, the feelings of teacher and students about each other, themselves, and what is going on;
4 the physical organization of the classroom;
5 the materials used in teaching;
6 the particular methodology employed by the teacher/in the materials.

and any other factors you consider to be relevant.

7.5 The Silent Way

The Silent Way (Gattegno 1972) is another set of techniques for language teaching that lays emphasis on affective factors of the teaching and learning situation. Here is a typical Silent Way classroom scenario:

The teacher and the students, about fifteen of them, are all seated around a table. The teacher puts a red wooden rod on the table and says 'a red rod' loudly and clearly. The teacher does the same with a blue rod, a green rod, and a yellow rod. The students watch and listen. The teacher then lifts the red rod from the table and points to one of the students. The student says 'a red rod'. The teacher nods, puts down the rod, picks up the green one, and points to another student. The student says 'a blue rod'. The teacher frowns and shakes his head. The student says nothing. The teacher points to another student, who provides the correct response. This continues for five or ten minutes. Then the teacher puts more red, green, blue, and yellow rods on the table and says, 'Give me a red rod.' One or two students reach hesitantly for a red rod, and the teacher motions in his own direction. One student hands him the wooden rod. The teacher points at that student and indicates all the rods on the table. The student says 'Give me a red rod.' The teacher picks up a red rod and hands it to her. He then points to another student and indicates one or two yellow rods on the table. The student says, 'Give me a yellow rod.' The teacher points to another student, who picks up a yellow rod and hands it to his classmate. Within a few minutes, the students are giving and taking rods among themselves without the need for prompting or intervention from the teacher at all.

▶ TASK 78

What do you think is the basic philosophy behind Silent Way lessons? Do you agree with it? Using the same points of contrast as

listed in Task 77 above, compare Silent Way with both Suggestopedia and Counselling Language Learning. What are the main
differences? What are the points of similarity, if any?

Taking another point of contrast, language level of students,
compare the three 'humanistic' techniques as regards their appropriacy for different levels, namely

1 beginners   3 intermediate
2 false beginners   4 advanced.

7.6 As a student: feeling and learning

The 'humanistic' techniques outlined above all have one thing in common.
They aim to make classroom learning more effective by influencing
affective factors in the classroom. Thus Suggestopedia aims to make the
learner feel more relaxed and less threatened. The Silent Way aims to make
the learner more independent and self-reliant. Both *Caring and Sharing* and
CLL aim to make the learner feel comfortable and accepted as a member of
a group.

 ## TASK 79

What are the basic assumptions behind these aims about the feelings
of learners in traditional, non-'humanistic' classroom situations?
Do you think these assumptions are justified? In your experience, do
learners in non-'humanistic' classrooms have these feelings?

Personal interaction in the classroom has already been mentioned in Unit 2
above. Students, like teachers, come to the language classroom with their
own personality characteristics. Some of their attitudes are due to their
basic dispositions and affect all areas of their lives. Some are due to the
learning experience, how they feel about the subject, the teacher, their own
progress, the particular classroom situation.

Here is a list of attitudes (from Stern 1983, Chapter 17) which research has
shown to have an important bearing on language learning:

1 *Authoritarianism*, unwilling to criticize authority, conformist.
2 *Ethnocentrism*, feeling one's own culture and community as superior.
3 *Anomie*, feeling dissatisfaction with one's own role in one's society.
4 *Perseverance*, willing to exert effort and not give up easily.
5 *Goal orientation*, having an aim in view, trying to achieve it.
6 *Introversion*, unwilling to mix with others, preoccupied with own
  thoughts.
7 *Extroversion*, willing to mix, be outgoing, take an interest in things and
  people.
8 *Infantilization*, feeling childish in a learning situation.
9 *Empathy*, willing to identify with others.

10 *Dependency*, feeling dependent on others.
11 *Tolerance of ambiguity*, willing to accept vagueness or lack of clarity.
12 *Self-criticism*, willing to criticize oneself.
13 *Status-consciousness*, unwilling to make a fool of oneself.

▶ **TASK 80**

1 Of this list of attitudes, which can be seen as

   a. preceding the classroom situation, and basic to the individual personality;

   b. engendered in the classroom, and brought about by the learning experience?

2 Of this list of attitudes, which do you think

   a. have a positive relationship with language learning;

   b. have a negative relationship with language learning?

Give reasons for your choice of (a) or (b) in both of the above questions.

Motivation clearly plays an important part in the formation of student attitudes in the classroom. Like the personality traits listed above, motivation can precede the classroom situation, or it can be engendered by it. The student can have strong reasons for wanting to learn a language before he or she ever comes to the classroom. In the course of attending a class strong reasons for continuing to attend and learn the language can emerge.

▶ **TASK 81**

Can you list the reasons a student might have for wanting to learn a language?

If a student is highly motivated to learn a language, will this have any implications for the teacher?

If a student is not motivated, what can the teacher do to engender motivation in him?

8 Describing classroom learning events

8.1 The pedagogic code: methodology

In Units 2 and 4, parallels were drawn between the use of language and the use of methodology in communicative situations, between the speech event and the learning event, between verbal interaction and pedagogic interaction. These parallels might usefully be taken further.

Every utterance in a speech event can be seen as consisting of two factors: propositional content and communicative purpose. The propositional content refers to those aspects of the real world that the speaker wishes to make reference to. The communicative purpose refers to the speaker's intentions in making the utterance, the effect he or she wishes to create in the hearer. (See Figure 14.)

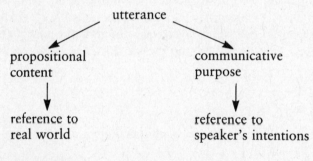

Figure 14

Thus in 'What are you laughing at, boy?', the content is the boy, his laughter, and the cause of his laughter. The purpose is to get the boy to stop laughing.

Similarly, every activity in a teaching event has the same two inherent factors. *Content* of a methodological activity is the syllabus item or teaching point, the aspect of real language the teacher wishes to make reference to. *Purpose* refers to the teacher's intention in employing the activity, the effect he or she wishes to create in the learner. (See Figure 15.)

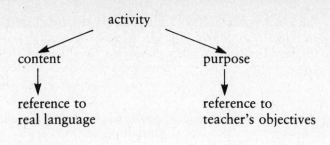

Figure 15

Thus in an activity like reading aloud by the teacher to the students, the content is text in the target language, maybe with structural or functional points of its own, depending on whether it is an authentic text, or a text devised specifically for teaching. The purpose is to get the students to listen and understand, if their books are closed, or to listen and look, if their books are open and the text available to them, matching the spoken with the written form.

▶ ## TASK 82

Study the following activities and see if you can describe the *content* and the *purpose* of each. The *purpose*, remember, refers to the teacher's objective in employing the activity. The *content* refers to the aspect(s) of real language, the syllabus item or teaching point, embodied in the activity. Thus the content of Activity 1 will be described in structural terms, the content of Activity 2 will be described in functional terms, and that of Activity 3 in skills terms.

1 Complete the following passage. The words in direct speech are listed at the foot of the passage:

I was walking down the road the other day when a man stopped me and asked the way to the nearest post office. I told him . . . (1), then . . . (2), where . . . (3) on the opposite side of the road. He asked me . . . (4) and I told him . . . (5). He thanked me and walked off.

1 'Take the first turning to the left.'
2 'Keep straight on till you reach the main road.'
3 'You'll see the post office facing you.'
4 'How far is it?'
5 'It's about half a mile at the most.'

(from Byrne 1965)

2 Find the difference

This game is played in pairs or in groups of four with two players per picture. Each player or pair of players has a picture. The pictures are identical except for a few differences. The players talk about their own picture until they have identified an assigned

number of differences. The number of differences they are asked
to identify is limited, in order to give the activity a goal, but the
players may go on talking when the two pictures are set side by
side.

(from British Council 1979)

3 Read this passage and complete the following diagram to show
the different stages of the wet process:

The wet process. First the fresh fruit is pulped by a pulping
machine. Some pulp still clings to the coffee, however, and this
residue is removed by fermentation in tanks. The few remaining
traces of pulp are then removed by washing. The coffee seeds are
then dried to a moisture content of about 12% either by exposure
to the sun or by hot-air dryers. If dried in the sun they must be
turned by hand several times a day for even drying.

(from Moore 1979)

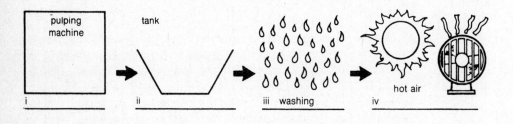

Figure 16

8.2 Using the code: activity sequences

In a lesson in the classroom, activities are joined together in a sequence.
Lesson plans outline a sequence of activities that the teacher intends to
follow. There are many accepted sequences, or routines, used in everyday
teaching practice. Most textbooks contain examples of such set procedures; many teacher trainers prescribe them.

Here are two examples of such commonly accepted activity sequences. The
first is for the presentation and practice of a new structure, such as the
Present Simple tense, or the use of 'how much/how many' with a class:

1 presentation of structure
2 repetition drill
3 substitution and/or transformation drills
4 written blank-filling exercise.

► TASK 83

Would this sequence of activities hold for all classroom contexts in which the new structure is to be presented? Consider, for example, a remedial class, where many students may already know the 'new' structure. How would you alter this sequence, if at all, for such a class?

Consider next a class which wants only a knowledge of the spoken language, not the written form. How, if at all, would you alter the activity sequence above for this class?

The second example of a commonly accepted activity sequence is this one for use with reading passages, normally in post-beginner and lower-intermediate classes:

1 Teacher reads text aloud. Students listen, books closed.
2 Teacher reads aloud again. Students listen and follow text in books.
3 Individual students read parts of the text. Teacher corrects.
4 Teacher asks questions on the text, following closely the wording in the text. Students find the answers in their books.

► TASK 84

This procedure is for reading passages. But does it actually involve the students in reading? Analyse the content and purpose of each activity in the sequence. State the learning effect of each activity, what the student actually gets out of it. How would you alter the activities/the sequence of activities to make it more relevant to reading?

Pre-set activity sequences are to be handled with caution. The nearest equivalent in verbal interaction is the phrase-book set of phrases or mini-dialogue. The phrase-book provides one scenario of how a conversation 'At the Chemist's', for example, might go. But in the real situation, the interaction might be somewhat different, and there is no guarantee that by sticking to the phrases outlined in the phrase-book, the speaker will achieve communication and get what he or she wants.

Similarly, in the classroom, the teacher must have an idea of what she intends to achieve, and how she intends to achieve it. But she must move activity by activity, judging how the interaction is going at each point. Pre-set sequences of activities may not always achieve the desired effect.

8.3 Interaction: lessons and conversations

In the lesson scenario given in 1.2, the teacher used a pre-set sequence of activities, without checking on or thinking about how these activities were actually engaging the students. This lesson was typified as an example of action and reaction, without any real interaction taking place.

▶ ## TASK 85

Study the following conversation. As a piece of verbal interaction, it has many features in common with the lesson from Unit 1 referred to above. What are the similarities between this conversation and the lesson in question?

Dental Receptionist: Good morning.
Young Man: Good morning. Can I see Mr Phillips, please?

D.R.: Have you see him before?
Y.M.: No, I haven't. I actually want to see him about . . .
D.R.: And are you in pain?
Y.M.: No, no. It's not that. You see, I . . .
D.R.: Well, if you aren't in pain, you'll have to make an appointment.
Y.M.: No, no. You don't understand. I . . .
D.R.: You can only see the dentist immediately if you're in pain. Otherwise, you need an appointment. Now, Monday at 10–10.30 is the earliest I can do for you.
Y.M.: I'm sorry, but I don't want to see him about . . .
D.R.: Name, please.
Y.M.: Yes. Tell him my name. It's John Roberts. Then he'll know I've come to see him about . . .
D.R.: Mr Roberts. Monday at 10.30. OK? Thank you.

And she shuts the glass partition between the receptionist's office and the waiting room. The young man stands confused for a moment. He had actually spoken to the dentist on the phone the day before and arranged to drop in and see him about training courses that his firm runs for dental nurses, receptionists, and assistants. He decides to move on to the next dentist in the street – this particular receptionist, after all, might just be too difficult to train!

In the same way, the features of other lesson types outlined earlier in this book can be found in many everyday conversations. The factors which make for successful or unsuccessful verbal communication are the same factors which lead to success or failure in classroom teaching.

8.4 The participants: teacher, student . . . and textbook

The ideal picture of classroom interaction is one of interaction between teacher and learners, as shown in Figure 17.

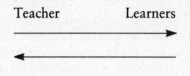

Figure 17

But, as was pointed out in 2.1 above, the textbook writer often becomes a participant in the interaction, albeit a more indirect one. If, for example, a very teacher-controlling textbook is in use, and if all the learners have access to a copy, then the normal pattern of interaction might look more like Figure 18 with no real teacher–learner interaction going on at all.

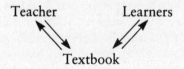

Figure 18

If the teacher is controlled by the textbook, but the school is poorly resourced, and the learners do not have access to a copy, then the pattern of interaction might deteriorate to that shown in Figure 19 with the teacher engrossed in the book, acting upon the learners as a result of his or her interaction with the book, and the learners left out of the interactive process altogether.

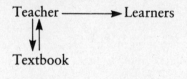

Figure 19

If the teacher uses the textbook from time to time, as one medium among others which can be employed to convey a pedagogic message, then the pattern of classroom interaction will vary during the course of the lesson, as the textbook, or the teacher's own activities, become the focus of the interaction at any given moment.

▶ TASK 86

Here is a short piece of classroom interaction from a lesson where a teacher is using a textbook as well as some ideas of her own to give her class practice in forms of requests.

First divide the piece of interaction into segments (see 2.2 above). There are three segments in it.

Then decide on the patterns of pedagogic interaction that are involved in each segment, and the different relationships between Teacher, Learner(s), and Textbook. Draw a diagram to illustrate each different pattern of interaction that you find.

T: OK I'd like you to look at page 47 now. At the first part. Can you see that yellow box at the top there? It shows you the two forms you've been looking at. 'Do you think you could come and look at it' and 'would you mind signing your name here please'. If you look at exercise 1 there they give you eight or nine situations. Some are formal some are informal. Now I'd like you to work two people together again, one person could make a request, for example, 'would you mind lending me your pen', and the other person would respond, 'certainly, here you are', or 'of course, here'. OK, so if you could just practise those nine situations, but remember please you must be sure are you speaking to a friend or are you speaking to an acquaintance or a stranger. OK.

Hilly: Do you think you could – could turn off the TV please.
Boujemaa: Of course.
Ghita: Could you turn the TV a little down.
Wafaa: A little.
Ghita: A little down.
Wafaa: Yes, of course.
T: OK excuse me – um – now our time is almost finished so I think I'd better take a register before we, before we go, would you mind lending me your pen a minute Hilly.
Hilly: Certainly.
T: Oh thank you very much. OK – um – Mekki are you here? Is Mekki here?
Mekki: Yes he is . . . yes I am.
T: OK . . . Yes I am – OK, and Asma.
S: No, she isn't.
T: Would you mind repeating that please.
S: No, she isn't here.
T: Ah she's absent is she? And Abdelmajid?
Abdelmajid: Yes . . . yes he is.
T: Good. Look Abdelmajid, would you mind finishing this for me while I get the next thing ready.

S: I am not Abdelmajid.

T: Oh Boujemaa excuse me, would you – would you mind finishing this for me.

Boujemaa: Of course.

T: . . . until I . . . the next bit . . . OK.

Boujemaa: Aziza.

S: She's absent.

Boujemaa: Absent.

Boujemaa: Who is this? And Anne-Marie. . . .

T: Thank you. OK before we finish then, I'd like to ask you to do something at home for tomorrow's lesson. If you could look at page 47 again at the six pictures. What you've got there are six situations, now I'd like you to write a short little dialogue, one for each of these pictures. OK? Now I don't only want the request I also want the – the answer, response. OK and please be very careful who the people are. Are they friends, are they strangers, do they work together, or whatever. OK? And we've got a minute left so perhaps before we go we can just have a look at the first picture together OK? So work in pairs again and just make a little dialogue for the first picture. All right. If you carry on.

Rene: Walter, could you give me my pen please.

T: Of course I could. Do excuse me.

Rene: Thank you.

S: Would you mind er . . .

Ghita: . . . my car please.

Wafaa: . . . would you . . . do you think you . . . do you think you could – er – er – help, help me in lifting my suitcase.

T: Time to go home, so remember to bring your homework with you tomorrow because we'll need it for the next lesson. OK. Thanks very much and see you tomorrow.

(British Council 1985)

Whoever the interactants in any communication situation may be, communication will be more easily achieved if they have a certain amount in common (see 2.1 above). Where the experience of the participants coincides, their experience of the world at large, of the particular aspects of it being referred to, and of the code being used for communicative purposes, then the chances of intention matching interpretation will be high.

Similarly, in the learning event, where the experiences of teacher and learners coincide, their experience of the world at large, of language in general and of classroom methodology, then the chances of teacher intention matching up with learner interpretation will be high. Everything the teacher does in the classroom will fulfil learner expectations.

Where there is a big difference between the experience and the expectations of the teacher and of the learners, in any or all of these areas, then there is potential for misunderstanding and lack of communication.

▶ TASK 87

Here are some learning events where misunderstanding occurs and communication is not successfully achieved. Explain why, in terms of the experience and expectations of the teacher and the learners:

1 A group of European secondary-school teachers are on a month's 'refresher' course in UK. They teach mainly grammar in their own schools, and use a national textbook which is based on passages for translation and grammar exercises. This is also the format of their national examinations in English. Their native-speaking tutor in the UK is convinced of the value of a functional approach to language teaching. He has therefore prepared for them a functional syllabus, with some skills work too. He wants them to get lots of oral practice, something they cannot get in their own countries. He spends the first morning working on different request forms . . . *Would you/could you/do you mind if* . . .; and the afternoon on communication games. The group is appalled. They go home angry and frustrated, wondering if this month will be worth their time and effort at all . . .

2 A teacher who has done a lot of work with young children goes into adult education for the first time. Her first group is a small group of ten academics from the Pacific Basin. They need to brush up their English before attending short courses in the UK on different scientific disciplines. The teacher realizes the need for variety and some physical stimulation during the long hours of tuition. She tries a few Total Physical Response exercises (that is, exercises which involve the students in physical reaction to her instructions). They are reluctant to participate. She goes home at the end of the first day wondering if all people from that part of the world are so grim and unco-operative . . .

3 A young American teacher has gone to teach university under-graduates in the Arab world. She is an expert in reading, having done a lot of research work on the use of word-attack skills, and the ability to précis passages by picking out the main points and condensing them, and has written a textbook on reading using this approach. She is constantly frustrated by her students' habit of memorizing everything they read, from word lists to whole passages. She tells them to stop, and gives them lots of practice in word-attack skills, such as guessing meaning from context, knowledge of prefixes and suffixes, and in reading for main points. She advocates these methods to improve reading, and

manages to get her book adopted for use throughout the university. But to no avail – they still memorize. She becomes convinced that her students are either intellectually sub-normal or being deliberately difficult, and plans to resign her job at the earliest opportunity.

In each case, what could have been done by (a) the teacher, (b) the students to prevent or repair the communication breakdown?

8.5 The setting: when and where

The use of the linguistic code is affected by the setting in which an utterance occurs, with regard to factors of time and place. Setting thus determines the appropriate use of 'come' and 'go', 'here' and 'there', 'then' and 'now', 'this' and 'that', 'last' and 'next'. It governs the utterance of 'Good morning', as opposed to 'Good evening'. It means that whereas 'Looks like rain' can be regarded as an appropriate conversation-opener in a temperate zone, it would hardly fulfil the same function in a tropical country in the middle of the monsoon season.

Similarly, the use of the methodological code is affected by the situation in which an activity occurs, the setting in physical and temporal terms. The teacher must take the setting into consideration when employing any methodological device.

Setting can be seen in immediate classroom terms, referring to the size, location, furniture, and resources of the room in which the class is located. Added to this would be temporal features as regards the time of day, the location of the particular lesson in the class day, the duration of the lesson, and so on.

▶ ## TASK 88

Consider in what ways the following types of classroom setting might influence or constrain the teacher's choice of methodological activities:

1 A large hall where five different classes are being held. No walls between the classes, only head-high cardboard partitions.
2 A classroom where both desks and benches are nailed firmly to the floor.
3 A classroom where only one textbook is provided for every six students.
4 A classroom with no electricity supply.
5 As at (4), at midday in the tropics.
6 A Friday afternoon, from 3 to 4 o'clock, towards the end of term.

TASK 89

Look again at the three different activities outlined in Task 82 above. What sort of classroom setting does each of these activities assume? Is there any way of adapting them for a more poorly-resourced setting than they assume?

Moving beyond the actual classroom, setting can also be seen as covering the more general area of school or educational institution in which the classroom in question is situated. The physical state of the school building and its location can be important. The general tenor of the school and the attitude of its headteacher can also have an effect. The curriculum and syllabus in use in the school is yet another influential factor at this level.

▶ **TASK 90**

How would the following affect the choice of methodological activities?

1 A school which practised strict discipline and a very authoritarian approach.
2 A headmaster who could not tolerate excessive noise in any of his classrooms.
3 A language department staff who all agreed on the 'communicative' approach to language teaching and dealt only with language functions in the classes.
4 An *ad hoc* 'school' under the trees in a tropical Third World village.
5 A school right next to a major international airport.
6 A curriculum geared tightly towards the needs and requirements of a final certificate examination.

At an even more remote level, yet one that informs those of both school and classroom, setting can be seen on a national or regional level. Thus a country's climatic and economic status has an important effect on what goes on in the individual classroom. A country's culture, the prevalent religion and political régime, have an important influence on the participants in that country's education system. They also tend to inform official national policies on education, and cultural views of what education should be.

▶ **TASK 91**

What effect do you think the following might have on language classroom interaction in the particular country concerned:

1 Tropical climate. Six months hot and dry, six months wet and humid. Diseases like malaria endemic to the population.

2 A political ambience where individuality is stressed. The rights of the individual are seen as more important than anything else.

3 A Third World economy. Desperate poverty and lack of resources. Education not seen as a priority.

4 A healthy economy. Education a priority, and a very high budget allocated to it. Almost limitless resources in educational technology.

5 Education seen as being a drawing-out of the individual, his or her own innate skills and abilities.

6 Education seen as being an instrument for the transference of cultural and social values, from one generation to the next.

Clearly, many of these factors interrelate. A country of low economic status will tend to have an education system geared to social development, rather than to individual development. It will also normally have poorly-resourced overcrowded classrooms, although it will still cater for a few élite and well-resourced institutions, as a rule.

The interrelationship of the many factors involved in setting can be seen in Table 6, where a few examples have been included under the various headings.

	Physical	Temporal	Psycho-social	Educational
Country/ region	Features of climate; economic status.	Ethos of 'the times' i.e. current trends and fashions.	Culture; religion; political régime.	Official policies on education; cultural views of education.
School/ educational institution	State of buildings; location; provision of resources.	Location in school year/ school term; timetabling.	School atmosphere; attitude of headteacher/ head of dept.	Location in curriculum; subject syllabus.
Classroom	Size; location; temperature; furniture; resources.	Location in class day; time of day; duration of lesson.	Class atmosphere; student/ teacher relationships.	Location in particular lesson/sequence of activities; scheme of work.

Table 6

All of these are factors which come to bear, in one way or another, on the appropriate choice of methodological activities in any given learning event. They are the factors of setting, the factors which root the event in the reality of the classroom situation.

Exploring

In this section you will have the opportunity to explore your own classroom and teaching situation, and to see how many of the ideas discussed in the first two sections of this book can apply to it. This is a section for action research: you are encouraged to identify problem areas in your own classroom, and to formulate possible solutions to the problems. Concepts and instruments which were outlined in Section One in the abstract, and applied to data from other people's classrooms in Section Two, are now to be applied to your own experience and everyday teaching activities.

It follows that a very high proportion of the tasks in this section require observation of actual classroom interaction. When your own classroom is involved, video or audio recordings of lessons will enable you to study your teaching in relative detachment. Video recordings are preferable to audio-recordings, since much more can be captured and observed in a visual medium. If you are working through this book with teacher colleagues, then much can be gained from observing each other's classes.

If you are not teaching, or if for some reason you are unable to observe colleagues' classes, then it should be possible to obtain recordings of classroom lessons to work on. Films and videos produced for teacher-training purposes contain many lengthy examples of authentic classroom interaction; most large teaching institutions, institutes of education, teachers' resource centres, and so on should have collections of recorded lessons. It should therefore be possible, whatever your situation, to obtain some sort of classroom data, and to adjust the following exercises where necessary in order to fit your circumstances. Although the tasks in this section are designed to be carried out by the individual teacher, the procedures can often involve colleagues, and the evaluation can be carried out in group discussion, so there are opportunities within tasks for teachers to work together on their professional development.

9 Exploring language in your classroom

9.1 Patterns of verbal interaction

These tasks are best done in sequence, in the order in which they appear here.

▶ TASK 92

Aim
To contrast patterns of verbal interaction employed in language lessons with those employed in other subject lessons.

Resources
- A language lesson, either a colleague's live lesson, or a recording of one of your own lessons.
- A lesson in another subject, such as science, mathematics, geography or history, from the same school/institution/area as the language lesson.

Procedure
First observe the language lesson, and note down the different patterns of verbal interaction that occur during the course of it, for example:

1 Teacher ⟶ Whole Class
2 Teacher ⟶ Individual Student
3 Individual Student ⟶ Teacher
4 Individual Student ⟶ Individual Student (as in pair-work)

and so on.

Then observe the other subject lesson and note down, in the same way, the different patterns of verbal interaction that occur during the course of that lesson.

Evaluation
Are your two sets of notes from the two different lessons similar, or are they significantly different? Was the pattern of verbal interaction much the same in the language class as it was in the other subject? Can you explain any similarities/differences?

Would you have expected the patterns of verbal interaction in the two classes to be the same or different? Justify your expectations.

What does this exercise tell you, if anything, about the language teaching and the teaching of the other subject that goes on in your school?

TASK 93

Aim
To contrast the patterns of verbal interaction employed in language lessons taught by different teachers.

Resources
Two language lessons, either live or recorded, either by two different teacher colleagues, or by a colleague and yourself, from the same institution/area.

Procedure
As in Task 92.

Evaluation
Are your two sets of notes from the two different lessons similar, or different? In either case, explain the similarities or differences.

Would you have expected the patterns of verbal interaction in the two classes to be the same or different? Justify your expectations.

What, if anything, did you learn about your own/your colleagues' teaching from this exercise?

TASK 94

Aim
To contrast patterns of verbal interaction employed in your own language lessons.

Resources
Two recorded lessons of your own, different in as much as they are
    a. with different classes; or
    b. based on different materials; or
    c. different in aim or content.

Procedure
As in Tasks 92 and 93 above.

Evaluation
Are your two sets of notes from the two different lessons similar, or significantly different? Can you explain any similarities or differences?

Would you have expected similar or different results from the two lessons? In either case, justify your expectations.

What, if anything, did you learn about your own teaching and classroom practice from this exercise?

9.2 Functions of classroom language

Tasks 95 and 98 are closely linked and should be done in sequence, if you wish to do all of them. Task 99 provides a lead-in to Task 100 in that it involves coding *part* of a lesson, rather than a whole lesson, according to the BIAS system. Task 101 cannot be attempted without previously completing either Task 99 or 100, nor can Task 102. It is possible to complete Tasks 99 to 102 before working on Tasks 95 to 98, rather than working straight through from 95 to 102.

 TASK 95

Aim
To contrast the language used in language lessons with the language used in other subject lessons, according to the Sinclair and Coulthard system.

Resources
– About ten minutes' worth of recorded classroom interaction from a language lesson. The equivalent amount of recorded classroom interaction from any other subject lesson in the same school/institution/area.
– The full set of Sinclair and Coulthard categories in 5.1 above.

Procedure
Analyse the language lesson excerpt into 'acts' and allocate the appropriate Sinclair and Coulthard category to each 'act'.

Then analyse and code the other subject lesson excerpt in the same way.

Evaluation
Is there any difference between the type of language coded according to the same category in the two different lessons? For example, compare 'elicitation' examples in the language lesson and the other subject lesson. Similarly, compare 'reply' and 'react' in the two lesson extracts.

If you can find any significant differences in these or other categories, how would you explain them?

▶ **TASK 96**

Aim
To contrast the language used in different types of language lesson, depending on whether the lesson is teacher-centred or student-centred.

Resources
– Two short recorded extracts, about 8 to 10 minutes in length, from two different language lessons. One should be of the teacher-centred variety, where the teacher is the central focus of the classroom activity, and the other should contain more student interaction in pair-work or group-work activities.
– The full set of Sinclair and Coulthard categories in 5.1.

Procedure
Analyse each extract into 'acts' and code the 'acts' according to the Sinclair and Coulthard system.

Evaluation
Is there any difference between the sort of language coded according to the same category in the two different lessons? For example, are the examples of 'elicitation' and 'informative' in the teacher-centred lesson in any way different from the examples of 'elicitation' and 'informative' in the student-centred lesson? What, if any, are the differences?

TASK 97

Aim
To see how applicable the Sinclair and Coulthard system of description is to your own teaching situation.

Resources
– The coded excerpts resulting from Tasks 95 and 96.
– The full set of Sinclair and Coulthard categories in 5.1.

Procedure
Examine the coded excerpts for any 'acts' you found it difficult to categorize according to the Sinclair and Coulthard system.

Evaluation
In the various excerpts you coded in Tasks 95 and 96, were there any utterances, any 'acts' for which you could not find a Sinclair and Coulthard category?

Are there any additional categories you would like to include in their system?

TASK 98

Aim
To see if the Sinclair and Coulthard system can usefully reveal anything about teaching, in addition to language used in classrooms.

Resources
– The coded excerpts resulting from your work on Tasks 95 and 96.
– If not included in the above, an excerpt from one of your own lessons, analysed and coded according to the Sinclair and Coulthard system.

Procedure
Examine the coded excerpts, at the same time thinking of what they represent in terms of teaching and learning.

Evaluation
Does the Sinclair and Coulthard analysis tell you anything significant about the sort of teaching going on in the lesson excerpts?

When one of your own lessons is analysed and coded according to this
system, can you learn anything from it about your own teaching and
classroom practice?

▶ ## TASK 99
Aim
To examine the use of language in one of your own lessons, using BIAS.

Resources
– The BIAS system of description outlined in 5.2 above.
– Some blank time-line displays on the model of Figure 20.
– Audio-recordings or video-recordings of two very different language-
  teaching activities, for example a structural or functional drill and a
  reading comprehension exercise, from a lesson or lessons of your own.

TL																								
TQ																								
TR																								
PR																								
PV																								
S																								
X																								

Figure 20

Procedure
Consider two different language-teaching activities that you normally
employ in your classes, for example a structural or functional drill and a
reading comprehension exercise, and draw up time-line displays for each of
the activities, showing the sort of pattern you think they normally follow.
The next time you actually teach the activities in question either

a. have them audio-recorded or video-recorded, and code them according
   to the BIAS system; or
b. have a colleague who is familiar with the BIAS system observe and code
   the activities for you as you teach them.

Whether (a) or (b) is employed, the result should be in the form of
completed time-line displays as illustrated in 5.2 above.

Evaluation
Compare the time-line displays based on your predictions with those based
on your actual teaching. Are there any significant differences between the
two? If so, can you explain them?

TASK 100

Aim
To examine the use of language in your own lessons, using the BIAS system.

Resources
- The BIAS system of description as outlined in 5.2 above.
- Time-line display sheets on the same model as those used in Task 99 above.
- Blank histograms on the model of those illustrated in 5.2 above.
- An audio-recording or video-recording of one of your own lessons.

Procedure
Take a lesson you are about to teach and draw up a histogram (see 5.2 above) to represent the way you think that the lesson will go in BIAS terms. For example, if you think, from your lesson plan, that there will be about fifty per cent TL, ten per cent TQ, ten per cent PR and so on, draw up a histogram accordingly.

When you teach the lesson, either

a. have it audio-recorded or video-recorded and then analyse the whole lesson according to the BIAS system; or
b. have a colleague who is familiar with the BIAS system observe and code the lesson as you teach it.

Draw up a histogram on the basis of the coded time-line displays produced by (a) or (b) above.

Evaluation
Compare the histogram of the actual lesson with the histogram of the lesson as you predicted it would go. Are there any significant differences? If so, can you explain them?

TASK 101

Aim
To see how applicable the BIAS system of description is to your own teaching.

Resources
The results of Task 99 and/or Task 100 above.

Procedure
Reflect on your experiences as you were coding the activities and/or lessons in the previous tasks.

Evaluation
Were there any parts of those activities or lessons you found difficult to code according to the BIAS system?

Are there any changes you would make or any other categories you would include in BIAS?

► TASK 102

Aim
To see what analysis of classroom language using BIAS can reveal about your teaching and classroom practices.

Resources
The results of Task 99 and/or Task 100 above.

Procedure
Examine the time-line displays and/or histograms produced by work on Task 99 and/or Task 100 above, at the same time reflecting on what you were trying to teach/achieve in those activities and/or lessons.

Evaluation
What, if anything, can you say that you learned about your own teaching from a BIAS analysis of it? Will you try to make any changes in your teaching as a result? What sort of changes?

9.3 Language in the language classroom

Tasks 103 to 105 deal with Bowers' categories of description for language classroom language (see 5.3 above), and should be done in the order in which they appear. Tasks 106 to 109 deal with Willis's categories from *Teaching English Through English* (see 5.4 above). It is possible to separate tasks 106 and 107 on social, personal, and organizational uses of classroom language from Task 108, on instructional classroom language. If Task 109 is to be attempted, however, with a comprehensive approach to all uses of language-classroom language, then it is necessary to complete all of Tasks 106 to 108 beforehand.

► TASK 103

Aim
To find out the proportion of mother tongue to target language you use in your own teaching.

Resources
– A lesson plan, and audio-recording or video-recording of the same lesson, taught by yourself.
– A blank pie-chart.

Procedure
Look at the lesson plan for a typical lesson in your teaching repertoire, say a drills and dialogue lesson, or exploitation of a reading text, or something similar. Estimate how much use of the mother tongue is normally made in the course of such a lesson, and fill in a blank pie-chart with your prediction of the relative proportions of mother tongue and target language.

When you teach the lesson in question, arrange to have it audio-recorded or video-recorded. From the recording, note down how many utterances in the lesson are in the mother tongue, whether these are teacher utterances or student utterances, and how many are in the target language.

Construct a pie-chart to show the relative proportions of mother-tongue use and target-language use. Then construct a pie-chart to show the relative proportions of teacher mother-tongue use to student mother-tongue use.

Evaluation
Is there any difference between your predictions of mother-tongue use and target-language use, and the actual proportions used in the recorded lesson?

Who uses the mother tongue most, yourself or your students?

 ## TASK 104

Aim
To analyse verbal behaviour in your classroom according to Bowers' categories.

Resources
- A lesson plan, and an audio-recording or video-recording of the same lesson taught by yourself.
- The complete set of Bowers' categories for verbal behaviour in the language classroom, as laid out in 3.3 above.
- Some blank pie-charts, on the same model as in Task 103 above.

Procedure
Take a lesson plan for a typical sort of lesson that you teach, like a reading comprehension exercise, or oral practice through role-playing, or something similar. Try to fill in a blank pie-chart according to Bowers' categories from your memories and impressions of how that particular lesson usually goes or should go. Think carefully about the proportion of silence in the lesson, the relative proportions of pupil-talk and teacher-talk and the proportions of the various functional categories that go to make up the verbal behaviour in the lesson. Look at the pie-charts in 5.3 as a model.

If you like, you can also fill in a smaller 'pie' with what you think the relative proportions of mother-tongue use and target-language use typically are.

When you teach the lesson in question, arrange to have it either audio-recorded or video-recorded.

From the recording, or transcript of the recording, code each utterance according to Bowers' categories, and note the use of mother tongue or target language for each.

After coding, calculate the approximate percentages for each category used. Fill in a pie-chart on the basis of these calculations, and a smaller pie-chart demonstrating the relative proportions of mother-tongue and target-language use.

Evaluation

How well do the pie-charts drawn up on the basis of memory and subjective impression match those drawn up on the basis of an actual lesson?

Are there are big differences between the two? If so, do these differences surprise you in any way?

What, if anything, have you learned from matching what really goes on in terms of verbal behaviour in one of your lessons with what you thought went on? Will you try to make any changes in your teaching or classroom practices as a result of this exercise? If so, what changes?

▶ TASK 105

Aim

To evaluate the BIAS and Bowers' systems of description.

Resources

Work on Tasks 103 and 104, and Tasks 99 to 102 above.

Procedure

Reflect on your experiences in implementing the BIAS and Bowers' systems in any or all of Tasks 99 to 104.

Reflect on what you learned about your classroom teaching from work on these tasks. This can form the basis of a small-group discussion where possible.

Evaluation

Of the two descriptive schemes, which did you find easier to implement? And why?

Of the two, which did you find more useful in telling you something about the sort of teaching and learning going on in your classroom? And why?

▶ TASK 106

Aim

To see what social, personal, and organizational uses are made of language in your own classroom/school/teaching institution.

Resources

– Five or six language lessons, either recordings of your own lessons, or a mixture of these plus lessons taught by your colleagues in the same school or institution.

– The following list (from Willis's *Teaching English Through English*) of the social, personal, and organizational uses of classroom language:

Beginning the lesson: Greetings; informal conversation, checking attendance.

Physical conditions: Comments on heat, light, noise, etc.

Getting organized: Seating arrangements; giving out books; getting blackboards cleaned, etc.

Different lesson stages: Introducing different activities in a lesson.

Using visual aids: Organizing and indicating them.

Using electrical equipment: Setting it up; apologizing if it won't work, etc.

Dividing the class up: Managing choral, team, group, pair, individual work.

Interruptions: Exploiting latecomers, things lost in the classroom, for brief conversations.

Control and discipline
Ending the lesson: Bringing things to a close; setting homework; tidying up.

Procedure

Observe the lessons, or recorded lessons, and note down any examples of verbal interaction in them that you consider not to be of a strictly pedagogic nature. Make a list of the other things that are talked about in the lessons apart from the topic or subject matter of the lesson itself.

Evaluation

How well does your list, derived from observation, match with Willis's list given above? Are there any significant differences? If so, what are they? Can you account for any of the differences between the two lists?

 ## TASK 107

Aim

To assess the relative proportions of mother tongue and target language used for social, personal and organizational purposes in your classroom.

Resources

- The list of examples of social, personal, and organizational uses of classroom language drawn up in Task 106 above.
- Willis's list given in Task 106 above.
- Three or four language lessons (colleagues' classes and/or recordings of your own classes).

Procedure

First, draw up a list of categories for the various non-pedagogic uses of classroom language, based on the list of examples and Willis's list from Task 106.

Using these categories, observe three or four language lessons, and, each time you observe a category from your list being used, note down whether it occurs in the mother tongue or in the target language. For example:

     Greetings: TL
     Attendance: MT
     Physical conditions: MT.

Evaluation
Can you make any generalizations, on the basis of these observations and notes, as to how the two languages are used in your classroom and/or school?

 TASK 108

Aim
To build up a comprehensive picture of instructional language use in your own teaching context.

Resources
The list of examples (below) of categories of instructional language, i.e. language used directly in the service of teaching activities and techniques (from Willis's *Teaching English Through English*):

Dialogues:
'The people in this dialogue are going to . . .'
'I want you to listen again, and this time, . . .'

Oral practice:
'Listen to this . . . Can you repeat it?'
'We're going to do a conversation drill. Look at these cues.'

Teaching vocabulary:
'Who knows what this word means?'
'You all know the word . . . Well, what's the opposite of it?'

Oral production:
'We're going to do some role play now. Suppose you were . . .'
'Look at these pictures of . . . Which do you prefer? Why?'

Listening skills:
'This is to give you practice in listening for . . .'
'Are you ready to listen and . . . I'll start the tape.'

Reading skills:
'Look at the title. What could this text be about?'
'The tenth line from the top. What does . . . refer to?'

Writing practice:
'Fill the blanks in these sentences and copy them neatly.'
'Check your punctuation.'

Written production:
'First you introduce the topic, then . . .'
'What type of words would be appropriate for this topic?'

You will need a few lessons, colleagues' classes or recordings of your own, each of a different type, from the list given above, for example:

— one lesson based on a dialogue
— one lesson based on listening work
— one lesson with a lot of vocabulary teaching in it.

Procedure

Observe the lessons and note down any instances of instructional language used by the teacher. Try to note down the exact words used by the teacher, and whether these are in the mother tongue or target language.

Evaluation

Do all your examples from observation and notes fit Willis's categories? Would you add more categories to the types of lesson activity given in Willis's list? Would you change any of the categories?

Could you draw up a list of categories, and examples of the instructional language used in each, based on the model of Willis's list, but drawn from your own specific teaching situation?

Are there any clear-cut patterns of mother-tongue and target-language use of instructional language in your notes? Do teachers in your context always use the mother tongue or the target language? Do they use a mixture? If so, is there any consistent pattern in the mixture?

 ## TASK 109

Aim

To evaluate language use in your own classroom/teaching context, and see if there is any room for improvement.

Resources

The picture of language use for (a) social, personal, and organizational purposes, (b) instructional purposes, and the picture of mother-tongue and target-language use, built up in Tasks 106 to 108.

Procedure

Examine the picture of classroom language use built up in the preceding three tasks to see if there is any room for improvement in this area of your classroom practice.

Evaluation

Are you satisfied with the picture of language use in your language classroom(s)? If so, justify your satisfaction.

Would you suggest any improvements to the current situation? If so, what? And what would be your reasons for making them? How would you go about making these improvements?

Will you personally make any significant changes in your use of language in the classroom as a result of these exercises?

The above questions could usefully provide discussion points for small-group discussion.

10 Exploring methodology in your classroom

10.1 Using observation instruments

Tasks 110 to 112 concentrate on applying the Mitchell and Parkinson descriptive instrument (see 6.2 above). Tasks 110 and 111 are independent of each other to the extent that 110 deals with 'segments' of a lesson, and 111 with actual lesson description in terms of the Mitchell and Parkinson categories. Task 112 cannot be properly attempted without first completing task 111. Tasks 113 to 115 deal with the TALOS observation instrument (see 6.4 above). Both Tasks 113 and 114 need to be completed before attempting the full-scale observation required in Task 115, but 114 could easily be done before 113, since each deals with a different section of the TALOS instrument.

▶ TASK 110

Aim
To understand the importance of structuring a lesson in segments, both in the planning and execution of the lesson.

Resources
- A lesson plan for a lesson you are about to teach.
- The list of Mitchell and Parkinson categories in 6.2 above.
- A recording of the lesson when you teach it, either audio or video.

Procedure
First take the lesson plan. Make sure it is clearly divided into segments, and try to describe each segment in terms of the Mitchell and Parkinson categories.

When you have taught the lesson, observe or listen to the recording of it. Without referring to your original work on the lesson plan, try to divide the recorded lesson into segments, and describe each of these segments in terms of the Mitchell and Parkinson categories.

Evaluation
How well does your analysis and description of the lesson plan match your analysis and description of the recorded lesson? Are there any big differences between the two? If so, can you account for these differences?

Did your detailed work on the lesson plan in any way influence how you actually taught the lesson?

Did you learn anything from this exercise in terms of either making lesson plans, or of actually teaching from them? If so, what exactly did you learn?

▶ TASK 111

Aim

To see what value the Mitchell and Parkinson observation instrument has for teacher-training purposes.

Resources
- A colleague's lesson, live or recorded.
- The Mitchell and Parkinson instrument as laid out in 6.2 above.

Procedure

Observe your colleague's lesson and analyse it according to the Mitchell and Parkinson system, coding each segment according to the appropriate categories.

Study the results of your observation, and decide how the teacher observed could best benefit from them. Note down any strengths or weaknesses in the teacher's handling of the lesson that you think are revealed by the observation data.

Now show your colleague (the teacher that you observed) the results of your observation. Explain if necessary the categories you used, but do not try to interpret them in terms of weak points or strong points of the lesson.

Once you are satisfied that your colleague fully understands the observation data, ask if he or she thinks they provide an accurate description of the lesson. Then ask your colleague to study the description and see if it can reveal anything about strengths and weaknesses in the lesson.

Evaluation

How well does your interpretation of the observation data match with your colleague's interpretation? Are there any significant differences of interpretation? If so, can you account for them or resolve them between you?

▶ TASK 112

Aim

To examine the sort of teaching that goes on in your school/institution, using the Mitchell and Parkinson instrument.

Resources
- Several different language classes in your school/institution, either live or recorded. These classes should cover a good spread with regard to teacher, level, content, and so on, so as to provide a representative cross-section of the sort of lessons taught in your school.
- The Mitchell and Parkinson instrument as laid out in 6.2 above.

Procedure

Observe the different language lessons, and code each of them according to the Mitchell and Parkinson instrument.

Evaluation

Do your observation data tell you anything about the sort of teaching that goes on in your school/institution? If so, what do they tell you?

Are there any clearly discernible patterns in the data? If so, what are they?

Do some descriptive factors appear consistently over the spread of different lessons? If so, which ones?

▶ **TASK 113**

Aim

To practise using the TALOS observation instrument.

Resources
– The TALOS low-inference section as presented in 6.4 above.
– At least twenty minutes' worth of a language lesson, live or recorded.

Procedure

First examine the TALOS low-inference section, and try to predict any difficulties that you might have in implementing this observation instrument in a classroom. Write down your predictions.

Now implement the instrument with a live class observation, or working on a recording. The check sheet provides for twenty minutes' worth of observation, i.e. 10 × 30 seconds out of every 120 seconds. When you are involved in coding the thirty seconds of lesson, you should fill in first the column headed by a number, i.e. (1). The subsequent columns headed by letters (a), (b), and (c) are only to be filled in if you need to mark an extra category or two for what goes on in the thirty seconds of observation time. For example, if, during the observation time, the teacher is primarily involved in *drill*, but also *corrects* a student, and has to *discipline* another, then the coding for that thirty-second period under *Teaching Act* will appear as shown in Table 7.

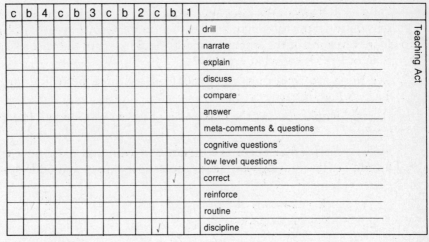

c	b	4	c	b	3	c	b	2	c	b	1		
											√	drill	Teaching Act
												narrate	
												explain	
												discuss	
												compare	
												answer	
												meta-comments & questions	
												cognitive questions	
												low level questions	
											√	correct	
												reinforce	
												routine	
										√		discipline	

Table 7

Continue coding the lesson from right to left of the check sheet in the same way until twenty minutes have passed.

Evaluation
What were the main difficulties you encountered in using TALOS?

Were the difficulties you actually had in implementing the system the same as those you predicted you might have?

 ## TASK 114

Aim
To become familiarized with the high-inference section of TALOS.

Resources
– The high-inference section of TALOS as laid out in Table 8 (taken from Ullman and Geva 1984). The various categories in this section are rated on a 0–4 scale, on the basis of subjective impressions accumulated throughout the lesson. Most of the categories refer to Teacher, and some to Student. The categories under 'Program' refer to the textbook, the course, the materials in use, and can be filled in at a remove from the classroom, simply by looking at these materials in the context of the general curriculum. The subjective impressions required to complete this section are meant to be gathered in the ninety seconds out of each two-minute period that the observer is not engaged in coding for the low-inference section of TALOS.

– A language lesson, either live or recorded.

Procedure
Observe the lesson, and when it is finished, turn to the TALOS high-inference check list (Table 8), and rate the lesson according to the categories given.

Evaluation
Did you find any of the categories more difficult to rate than others? If so, why do you think this might be? Are there any categories you consider to be more revealing of the strengths and/or weaknesses of the lesson observed than others? If so, what are they?

Are there any important categories you feel have been left out of the TALOS high-inference section?

Overall, would you say the lesson you observed was a good, fair, or bad one?

How do each of the categories correlate with your overall judgement of the lesson, i.e. do the following scores necessarily imply a good lesson?

> Use of L1: 0
> Teacher humour: 4
> Student participation: 3

Table 8

TEACHER	extremely low	low	fair	high	extremely high
Use of L 1	0	1	2	3	4
Use of L 2	0	1	2	3	4
teacher talk time	0	1	2	3	4
explicit lesson structure	0	1	2	3	4
task orientation	0	1	2	3	4
clarity	0	1	2	3	4
initiate problem solving	0	1	2	3	4
personalized questions and comments	0	1	2	3	4
positive reinforcement	0	1	2	3	4
negative reinforcement	0	1	2	3	4
corrections	0	1	2	3	4
pacing	0	1	2	3	4
use of audio-visual aids	0	1	2	3	4
gestures	0	1	2	3	4
humour	0	1	2	3	4
enthusiasm	0	1	2	3	4

STUDENTS					
Use of L 1 on task	0	1	2	3	4
Use of L 2 on task	0	1	2	3	4
student talk time on task	0	1	2	3	4
initiate problem solving	0	1	2	3	4
comprehension	0	1	2	3	4
attention	0	1	2	3	4
participation	0	1	2	3	4
personalized questions and comments	0	1	2	3	4
positive affect	0	1	2	3	4
negative affect	0	1	2	3	4
S to S interaction on task	0	1	2	3	4

PROGRAM					
linguistic appropriateness	0	1	2	3	4
content appropriateness	0	1	2	3	4
depth	0	1	2	3	4
variety	0	1	2	3	4
listening skill focus	0	1	2	3	4
speaking skill focus	0	1	2	3	4
reading skill focus	0	1	2	3	4
writing skill focus	0	1	2	3	4
formal properties	0	1	2	3	4
functional properties	0	1	2	3	4
integration with general curriculum	0	1	2	3	4

► TASK 115

Aim
To assess the value of the TALOS instrument for teacher-training purposes.

Resources
- The TALOS low-inference and high-inference sections as laid out in 6.4 and in Task 114 above.
- At least thirty minutes' worth of a language lesson, live or recorded.

Procedure
Try to apply both parts of the TALOS instrument to the lesson you observe, following the intended procedures of thirty seconds' low-inference coding followed by ninety seconds' high-inference impression-gathering in every two-minute period. Fill in the low-inference check sheet as you observe, and the high-inference check list once the observation is finished.

Evaluation
Looking at both sets of observation data, from the low-inference and high-inference sections of TALOS, how do you think you could use them to assess the classroom performance of the teacher observed?

In what way does each set of data reveal strengths and weaknesses in the lesson observed?

10.2 Raising teacher awareness

The following four tasks all explore ways in which simple observation exercises and instruments can be useful in making teachers think about their own classroom practice. The first two concentrate on error correction, and should be attempted in the order in which they appear. Task 117 is quite independent of the preceding two, and gives an opportunity to try out work done in 6.5, in the context of your own classroom. The final task is a more general one and can again, if wished, be done in isolation from the preceding tasks.

► TASK 116

Aim
To explore your own practice with regard to error correction in class, through introspection and observation.

Resources
- A list of the methods you think you normally use to correct errors made in oral work during the course of a lesson.
- A few recorded lessons of your own classes.

Procedure
First think about your own classroom practice. Have you listed all the methods you use to correct errors in oral work? Are you sure which

methods you use most often? What is your attitude to error correction in class? Do you correct all errors as/after they occur? Do you let some pass, feeling that to correct the student might inhibit fluent production?

Make a note of all these aspects of error correction. Then observe two or three recorded lessons of your own. Note your attitude to error correction in these lessons, and any methods of error correction that you use. Also note how many errors you correct, and how many you let pass.

Evaluation
Do the data from your observations match the notes you made prior to observation? Does your actual classroom practice accord with your stated attitude to error correction? Are there any significant differences between the two? If so, what are they?

TASK 117

Aim
To use observation exercises to raise teacher awareness in your school/institution in the field of error correction.

Resources
– The observation instrument on error correction given in 6.5 above.
– The results of Task 116 above.
– Language lessons taught by your colleagues, either live or recorded.

Procedure
First look at the observation instrument outlined in 6.5 above. If necessary, extend it to include any further categories of error correction in your own practice revealed by your work on Task 116 above.

Then use the observation instrument on some of your colleagues' classes. Show the data resulting from your observations to the teachers you observed. Find out from them if the information about their error correction practice in class is helpful to them in any way.

Evaluation
What did your observations reveal about error correction methods used by individual teachers you observed? What did they reveal about error correction methods used in your school or teaching institution as a whole?

Did the teachers you observed find the results of your observations useful to them? If so, in what ways were they useful?

Have you personally changed your methods of, and/or your attitude to, error correction in class as a result of these two tasks? If so, what changes have you made, and why?

▶ TASK 118

Aim
To try out and develop a simple observation exercise designed by yourself.

Resources
- The observation exercise you designed in Task 66 above.
- An appropriate lesson, live or recorded, to use the observation exercise on. (Don't choose a teacher-centred lesson based on reading or translation in order to try out an observation exercise on pair-work and group-work activities, for example.)

Procedure
Observe the lesson and apply the observation exercise.

Evaluation
Did the observation instrument work? If not, why not?

Could the instrument be improved? If so, in what way(s)?

Redesign your observation instrument on the basis of your actual experience in trying to implement it.

▶ TASK 119

Aim
To develop observation exercises to raise teacher awareness in your own teaching context.

Resources
- Observations made, in the course of all the previous tasks, of your own teaching and that of your colleagues.
- Language lessons, live or recorded, taught by yourself and your colleagues.

Procedure
Note down any particular areas of teaching that you have identified from previous observations as being in need of improvement. Think of any pedagogic areas where teacher awareness needs to be raised as regards

1 yourself and your own teaching
2 the teaching of particular colleagues
3 general teaching practice in your school/teaching institute/town/region.

Once you have identified areas in need of treatment under these three headings, devise observation exercises, along the lines of that in Task 66 above, that will serve to focus attention on them. Try these exercises out in order to judge their feasibility and effectiveness.

Evaluation
How well did the exercises work? What changes did you have to make to them as a result of actually trying to implement them?

Has teaching in the target areas improved or changed in any way as a result of applying the observation exercises you devised?

10.3 Finding out about the learner

Tasks 120 and 121 are similar, and you can attempt either or both of them in any order. Task 122 concentrates on more detailed areas of methodology, and should be completed before Task 123 is attempted. The next task treats a very different area, that of learning strategies, and the final task, Task 125, includes elements of all five preceding tasks, and should therefore be done only after the others are all completed.

Use the mother tongue in these tasks.

 TASK 120

Aim
To find out what your students are learning.

Resources
A small piece of paper for every student in the class.

Procedure
At the beginning of a language lesson, ask all the students to think about their last language lesson with you. Ask them to write down in their mother tongue what they learned in that lesson. Emphasize that you want replies along the lines of:

> 'I learned that . . .'
> 'I learned how to . . .'

and not blanket generalizations such as:

> 'I learned the Past Simple tense'.

Give the students five minutes to complete this exercise, and then gather in their replies.

Evaluation
How did the students' view of what they learned compare with what you intended them to learn in the lesson in question? Were there any big differences between what you taught, and what they learned? What were the differences, if any? Can you account for them?

 TASK 121

Aim
To see if your students are learning what you are teaching.

Resources
A small piece of paper for each student in the class.

Procedure
Leave five minutes free at the end of a language lesson. Tell the class:

> 'In this lesson I aimed to teach you . . . (state a number: one, two, three) things. What do you think they were?'

The students can write the answers (in their mother tongue), as in the previous task, or they can produce them orally. You may need to help the students with a prompt such as:

You taught us that (1) ....
     and that (2) ....
     and how to (3) ....

Evaluation
How well do the student replies match your teaching objectives for the lesson? Are there any big differences between the two? If so, what are they? How can you account for any differences that appear?

▶ TASK 122

Aim
To find out how students feel about your error-correction practice in the classroom.

Resources
A questionnaire devised to get student reaction to your normal error-correction practice, for example a mother-tongue version of the following:

When the teacher corrects students' mistakes in oral work, he/she corrects them by
a. repeating the mistake after the student
b. asking another student if what has been said is correct
c. making a face to indicate that the student has made a mistake
d. telling the student that he or she has made a mistake
e. telling the student what area the mistake is in—e.g. tense, pronunciation, etc.

Which of these methods do you like most . . . and why...
....
Which of these methods do you like the least . . . and why ....
....
Do you prefer the teacher to correct every mistake you make? Or do you prefer to have only the important mistakes corrected? ....
Give reasons for your answer ....
....

The above can be adapted to suit your own practice.

Procedure

Get your students to give their responses to the questionnaire in class. They can be encouraged to discuss the questionnaire in small groups before filling it in individually.

Evaluation

Read the completed questionnaires to see how the students feel about this area of your methodological practice. Is your current practice satisfactory as far as your students are concerned?

Could you change your error-correction practice to suit your students better? If so, in what way(s)?

▶ TASK 123

Aim

To find out how students feel about different areas of your methodological practice.

Resources

Short questionnaires in the mother tongue, similar to the example in the preceding task, on other areas of your methodological practice. For example, questionnaires:

a. to find out if the students understand the point of pair-work, and how much benefit they feel they get from it (or group-work);
b. to find out if the students understand why they do different types of reading comprehension task, and which types they find most useful (or types of listening comprehension task, drill, and so on);
c. to find out if the students really need variation of activity in a lesson, and if so, just how much they need.

Procedure

Try out the questionnaires with your students to see if they provide you with the sort of information you want. Make any necessary revisions or adaptations in them until you get the information you need.

Evaluation

What have you learned about your teaching as a result of each of the questionnaires you devised and had completed by your students?

▶ TASK 124

Aim

To find out what learning strategies are used by your students.

To familiarize your students with different learning strategies they might use.

Resources

The list of learning strategies given in 6.7 above.

Procedure

First make sure your students understand exactly what is meant by each of the strategies on the list. Then discuss with the students, or organize group discussion among the students, about which of the strategies they think they use in their own language learning. Get them to add to the list any other strategies they think they might use. Ask them to differentiate, if possible, between strategies used for learning in the classroom situation, and strategies used for learning at home.

Evaluation

Are you surprised by any of the strategies your students say they use? Which ones? And why?

Will you/can you alter your teaching practice in any way to exploit the learning strategies your students employ?

▶ TASK 125

Aim

To keep in touch with your students' learning through learner diaries.

Resources

A small notebook for each student in the class. The work you have done on Tasks 120 to 124 above.

Procedure

Give the students five minutes at the end or beginning of lessons to make notes in the mother tongue on what and how they learned in that lesson or the previous one. These notes should be kept in a notebook specially for the purpose, and should be seen as an extension of the sort of work done in tasks.

Students should be encouraged to note down points of obscurity and confusion, as well as instances of successful learning. This diary-keeping can be extended in time to periods of language work at home, students noting down in the same way what and how they learned from homework exercises and assignments.

Take in these diaries every so often, say once every two or three weeks, and leaf through them.

Evaluation

How well do accounts of learning in the student diaries match your own teaching plans? Are the students learning what you want them to learn? Are they learning in the way you expect them to learn? If not, how can you resolve the differences?

11 Exploring affect in your classroom

11.1 The observables

The tasks here can be done in any order, and need not be attempted in the sequence in which they appear. Tasks 127 and 129 focus on the teacher's view of things in the classroom, and Tasks 128 and 130 on the learners'. It is, however, important that all the tasks be completed if a full picture of affective factors in the classroom is to be built up.

 ## TASK 126

Aim
To see if affective factors in the classroom situation can be 'objectively' observed.

Resources
– The results of your work on Task 74.
– A live or recorded language lesson.

Procedure
In Task 74, you were asked to consider positive and negative manifestations of affect in the classroom under three main headings:

> general classroom atmosphere
> teacher attitude and behaviour
> student attitude and behaviour.

Now turn the features you listed under these headings into categories for observation under the same headings. Then observe a lesson and mark the presence or absence of features according to your observation categories.

Evaluation
How does this 'objective' marking of observation categories relate to your subjective impressions of the class atmosphere, and teacher and student behaviour, in the lesson you observed?

Do they provide the same type and amount of information as can be gathered by subjective impressions?

TASK 127

Aim
To match an observer's views of a lesson with the teacher's views.

Resources
A language lesson taught by one of your colleagues.

Procedure
Observe your colleague's class and note down your impressions of affective features of the lesson, based either on observation categories such as those you used in Task 126 above, or impressions that are purely subjectively gathered. These should be impressions of how the teacher felt/behaved during the lesson, and how the students felt/behaved, and of how the general class atmosphere felt, and so on.

At the end of the lesson, ask the teacher you observed to note down in the same way his or her impressions of how the lesson went, i.e. treating his or her own attitude and behaviour during the lesson, those of the students, and the general class atmosphere.

Evaluation
Compare your notes with those of the teacher observed. How well do they match? Where are the main similarities and/or differences between the two? Can you account for any differences?

TASK 128

Aim
To match an observer's views of a lesson with the student's views.

Resources
– A language lesson taught by one of your colleagues.
– A piece of paper for each student in the class.

Procedure
Observe your colleague's class and record your impressions of affective features of the lesson as in Task 127 above.

Arrange with the teacher to stop the lesson five minutes before time is up, and use that five minutes to get students' impressions of how the lesson went. Ask students to write down:

1 How they felt during the lesson (bored/interested/angry/amused or whatever) and why.
2 How they think the teacher felt during the lesson, and on what evidence they base their impressions.
3 How they would describe the general class atmosphere during the lesson (tense/relaxed, friendly/boring or whatever).

   Give the students time to write their answers to these three questions, and then collect them in.

Evaluation
Compare your notes on the lesson with the students' answers to the questions you asked. How well do they match? Where are the main similarities and/or differences between the two? Can you account for any differences?

 TASK 129

Aim
To find out how other teachers judge affective factors in a classroom.

Resources
As many practising teachers, of any subject, as you can make contact with.

Procedure
Find out from these teachers (either (1) by getting their written response to a simple questionnaire or (2) through informal discussion with them) on what evidence they tend to base a general feeling about any class they are teaching; how they can tell, for example, if a class is bored/interested/confused/restless, and so on.

Then find out if the same features are applicable to individuals within their classes; how teachers know, for example, whether a specific individual student is bored/confused/restless/interested, and so on.

Evaluation
Are there any features common to a large proportion of the teachers' answers? Can you make any generalizations about observable signs of affect in a class from this piece of simple research?

 TASK 130

Aim
To find out how students judge their teachers in terms of affective factors.

Resources
As many students, in as many different classes, as you can make contact with.

Procedure
Find out from these students (either (1) by written responses to a simple questionnaire or (2) through informal discussion) on what evidence they base judgements about a teacher's character and attitudes; how they can tell, for example, if a teacher is strict/relaxed/good-natured/easy-going/in a bad/good mood, and so on.

This information should always be gathered when the students' normal class teacher is not present.

Evaluation

Are there any points common to a large proportion of the student responses? Can you make any generalizations about observable signs of affect in a teacher from this piece of simple research?

11.2 The teacher

Many of the points in the following five tasks also arise in the book in this series on teacher and learner roles. Further reference should be made to this book if you wish to follow up any of the lines of thought started in these tasks. The tasks can be done in any order, and you need not follow through the sequence as it appears here. You may, in fact, wish to select only one or two tasks in areas which interest you.

▶ TASK 131

Aim

To clarify your own ideas about the teacher's role in the classroom.

Resources

A quiet half-hour in which to reflect on your own experience and practice.

Procedure

Ask yourself how you see the teacher's role in the language class; what image of yourself you try to convey to your students; how you want your students to see you. Think in terms of:

> personality
> social relations with class
> discipline and control
> pedagogic role.

Write down a brief description of how you see your role as a teacher as a result of your thought and reflection here. This written description can form the basis of small-group discussion if you are working with teacher colleagues.

Evaluation

How easy was it to describe your role? Were there any particular areas you had difficulty with, or any areas you had to think especially hard about? If so, what were they?

▶ TASK 132

Aim

To examine your own assumptions about the role of the teacher.

Resources

Four or five language lessons taught by teachers other than yourself.

Procedure
Observe the lessons, and take notes to describe the personality of each of the different teachers you observe. Once you have observed all the lessons, try to identify, out of all the teachers observed, one as the 'best' teacher and one as the 'worst' teacher. Try to provide reasons for your choice.

Evaluation
Which personality description correlates with your 'best' teacher? And which is that of your 'worst' teacher? Do you think the personalities involved influenced your judgement of 'best' and 'worst' in any way? If so, in what way?

▶ TASK 133

Aim
To examine your own expectations of student behaviour.

Resources
A quiet half-hour for reflection.

Procedure
Ask yourself how you expect students to behave in your classroom. Think in terms of their attitudes and behaviour towards:

> yourself, the teacher
> the lesson in hand
> learning the language, at home and in class
> each other, their fellow-students.

Write down a brief description of your expectations of student behaviour as a result of your thought and reflection here. This written description can form the basis of small-group discussion if you are working with teacher colleagues.

Evaluation
How well do your expectations of student behaviour match the way students actually behave in your classes? Where are the main similarities and/or differences? If there are differences, can you account for them?

▶ TASK 134

Aim
To see how applicable the 'humanistic' approaches are to your own teaching situation.

Resources
The outlines of the various 'humanistic' approaches in 7.3, 7.4, and 7.5 above.

Procedure
Consider the various 'humanistic' approaches outlined in Unit 7 in the light of your own classroom. Ask yourself which of the three (the Silent Way, Suggestopedia, Counselling Language Learning) you would feel most comfortable with in your own classroom, and why; and which of the three you would feel least comfortable with, and why. If you are working with teacher colleagues, these questions could form the basis of small-group discussion.

Then consider whether you could use any parts of any of these approaches in your day-to-day teaching. If so, which parts? How would you make any necessary adaptations in the approach and/or in your own teaching routines?

Evaluation
Try out your ideas in class, using either an unmodified humanistic approach if it seems feasible, or an adapted approach, or selected features from any or all of the approaches described. How well, or badly, do they work in class?

 **TASK 135**

Aim
To see if 'humanistic' exercises can be used in your own teaching.

Resources
The exercise from *Caring and Sharing in the Foreign Language Classroom* given in 7.2 above.

Procedure
First ask yourself whether you could use this exercise in one of your classes and if so, why; if not, why not. Try to predict class reaction to the exercise. If you are working with teacher colleagues, these questions could usefully form the basis of small-group discussion.

Evaluation
Try the exercise out in class, if you feel it is at all possible, making any adaptations you feel necessary. How does class reaction to the exercise match your predictions?

11.3 The student

Tasks 136 and 137 are directly concerned with teacher and student roles, and reference must again be made to Tony Wright's volume on that subject in this series. Task 138 explores student attitudes to the language being learned, and Task 139 their motivation for learning it. Task 140 explores student attitudes to learning, and Task 141 is concerned with the correlation between attitudes and performance. Tasks 136 and 137 are therefore in some respects different from Tasks 138 to 141, and 138 need not be done in sequence after 137. There are no strict rules governing the order that tasks should follow here, except that Task 141 would be more usefully done after Tasks 138 to 140 have been completed.

 ## TASK 136

Aim
To find out what your students' views of the teacher's role are.

Resources
– Several classes of students, your own or colleagues'.
– Your work on Tasks 131 and 132 above.

Procedure
Try to find out in any of the following ways what student expectations of the teacher are:

1 Ask the class to write a short composition or paragraph on a theme such as: 'The best teacher I had at Primary/Secondary School' (whichever preceded the current institution) or 'The worst teacher I had at Primary/Secondary School'.

2 Organize a formal class debate along the lines of: 'Teachers should be strict' versus 'Teachers should be relaxed and friendly'.

3 Devise a questionnaire to give to your students. In order to ensure frank answers, it should be administered by someone other than the normal class teacher, and strict anonymity should be preserved when the questionnaires are returned. As well as covering aspects of teaching competence, the questionnaire can cover areas of personality, for example:

Do you like a teacher who is
a. a strict disciplinarian
b. tolerant of all sorts of behaviour
c. strict on some occasions, tolerant on others, etc?

Do you like a teacher who is
a. lively and enthusiastic
b. quiet and serious
c. friendly and taking a personal interest, etc?

The questionnaire can also ask for opinions in a more direct way, for example:

Who is/was your favourite teacher? Why?
Which teacher do/did you like least? Why?
Whose classes do/did you enjoy most/least? Why?

The method used to obtain students' views will depend very much on the level of the class involved, and the amount of time available for the activity you want to employ.

Evaluation

Once you have gathered sufficient students' views on the role of the teacher, match them against the results of your work on Tasks 131 and 132 above. How well do your views and your students' views coincide? Where are the main similarities and/or differences between the two? Are you surprised by any of the differences, if there are any?

 ## TASK 137

Aim

To find out how students see their own role in the classroom.

Resources

- Several classes of students, either your own or colleagues'.
- The results of your work on Task 133 above.

Procedure

Try to find out what the students' expectations are as regards themselves in the classroom. This can be done, as in Task 136, by any of the following methods, dependent on the level of class, and the time available.

1 Composition or paragraph-writing on the theme of 'good' and 'bad' students, for example:
'I think I am a good/bad student because . . .'
'X is the student I admire most/least in class because . . .' and so on.

2 Discussions or formal debates on topics like:
'Teachers know best . . . or do they?'
'Do learners really need teachers?'
'Happy classes learn best.'
'Hard work is the only way to learning success'
and so on.

3 A specially devised questionnaire to gather information and opinions from students in the following areas:

   a. the most desirable student behaviour in the classroom;
   b. the most desirable classroom atmosphere for effective learning;
   c. relationships between learners and teachers in both social and pedagogic terms;
   d. the degree to which students should be dependent on teachers
   and so on.

Evaluation

Once sufficient information on students' views of themselves has been gathered, match it against the results of your work on Task 133 above. How well do your views and your students' views of their role in the classroom coincide? Where are the main similarities and/or differences between the two? Are you surprised by the differences, if there are any?

▶ **TASK 138**

Aim

To find out how your students feel about the language they are learning.

Resources

– Several classes of students, your own and/or colleagues'.
– Ten–fifteen minutes' time for informal discussion in each class.

Procedure

Gather as many value judgements from students as you can, by holding informal classroom discussions with them about the language they are learning, for example:

a. Is it ugly or attractive to listen to?
b. Is it difficult or easy to use?
c. Is it more/less attractive/complex/interesting/logical, etc. than their native language?

Ask them about the culture to which this language belongs, for example:

a. What kind of people do you think X-speakers are?
b. Would you like an X-speaker as a friend?
c. Would you like to meet some X-speakers?
d. Do you think X-speakers are more/less friendly/serious/hard-working/ fun-loving/etc. than yourselves?

Try to get students to justify their opinions where possible, but concentrate on the initial value judgements, and note down as many of them as possible in the course of discussions.

Evaluation

Can you make any generalizations from the information you have gathered? How do your students feel in general about the language they are learning? And the people who speak it? Do you share their feeling? Are you in any way surprised by their feelings?

▶ **TASK 139**

Aim

To find out about your students' motivations for learning the language.

Resources

– Several classes of students, either your own or colleagues'.
– A small piece of paper for each student.
– Ten minutes of class time.

Procedure

Ask each student to write down his or her replies to the following two questions:

1 Are you very/only moderately/not very interested in learning to speak/read/write/understand X well?
2 What are the reasons for the answers you gave to the question above?

Collect in all the responses.

Evaluation

Can you make any generalizations from the responses you have collected? Are students well or poorly motivated to learn the language? What, if anything, does motivate them to learn?

If they seem unable to find good reasons for learning the language in question, then it is essential to hold informal discussions in class on the basis of their responses. Reasons for learning the language should be discussed openly with the students.

► ## TASK 140

Aim

To find out how students feel about the learning experience in your classroom.

Resources

— Several classes of students, your own or colleagues'.
— About thirty minutes' time with each class.

Procedure

Begin a class discussion on how people can feel in a classroom learning situation, and introduce a few relevant adjectives, for example: *dependent, childlike, frustrated*, and so on.

Once you feel the students are clear about what you are trying to describe, put them into small groups of four or five, to discuss in their native language their own feelings about learning in the classroom, and to produce some relevant adjectives. Each group is expected to produce a list of adjectives. Dictionaries should be available so that these adjectives can be presented in the target language. After ten minutes or so, stop the work, and ask each group for its adjectives. List these on the board, and discuss each one with the class in turn to find out if the whole class shares this feeling, or if it is specific to one or two individuals.

Evaluation

Can you make any generalizations from trying out this activity with a few classes? How do your students/students in your institution generally feel about the classroom learning experience? Are there any other important factors influencing their feelings, for example the teacher they are learning with, the subject matter, and so on?

▶ TASK 141

Aim
To see how learner attitudes correlate with learner performance.

Resources
– A class of students you know really well.
– The list of learner attitudes given in 7.6 above.

Procedure
Look at the list of learner attitudes, and consider them in relation to individual students in your class. List against each student's name the different attitudes from the list that he or she displays. Then consider how the attitudes listed for each student correlate with that student's overall performance in learning the language.

Evaluation
Can you make any generalizations on the basis of the above? Are there any attitudes consistently displayed by the better students? And any by the weaker? Does there seem to be any pattern of correlation at all between student attitude and student performance?

12 Exploring learning events in your classroom

12.1 Methodology

Task 142 is concerned with lesson planning. Tasks 143 to 145 focus on the execution of the lesson plan, and the potential gap between what is taught and what is learned. Task 142 should therefore precede the others. Task 145 is in many ways an alternative to Task 144, although both procedures could well be used on the same lesson, with possibly interesting results.

 TASK 142

Aim
To see how well planned your lessons are.

Resources
A lesson plan, or a textbook lesson you often use, or a recording of one of your own lessons.

Procedure
Take the plan/lesson you have taught and analyse the individual activities in it, according to the content and the purpose of each one (see 8.1 above).

After doing this exercise with a few lessons of your own, try it with lessons of your colleagues, or of other teachers.

Evaluation
Did you find any activities where the content and/or purpose was not immediately clear? Would you change these activities in any way now if you were to teach the lesson again?

Did you find that thinking in terms of activity content and purpose sharpened your approach to lesson planning in any way? If so, in what way?

 TASK 143

Aim
To see how lesson plans can change in the classroom, and for what reasons.

Resources
– A lesson plan, or a textbook lesson you have prepared.
– A recording of the lesson when you actually teach it.

Procedure
Match the lesson plan with the recording of the actual lesson and make a
note of any divergences, however small, from the plan.

Evaluation
How closely did the lesson follow the plan? Can you say why the classroom
lesson diverged from your lesson plan, when (and if) it did?

Do you think these divergences were in any way predictable before you
started to teach the lesson?

 ## TASK 144

Aim
To see to what extent teaching in a lesson matches the learning that takes
place as a result of it.

Resources
– A lesson plan or a textbook lesson you have prepared.
– A recording of the lesson when you actually teach it.

Procedure
First take the lesson plan, and analyse the sequence of activities in the plan
according to the teaching acts (see 8.1–8.2 above) they represent. Note
down the teaching objective, the pedagogic intention, behind each activity
in the lesson.

Then observe the recording of the lesson as it is executed in the classroom,
and this time analyse the sequence of activities according to the learning
effect they produce. Note down what the learners seem to get out of each
activity. (Also see 4.5.) Sometimes you may not be sure what the learning
effect is. A reaction of silence, for example, tells the observer nothing about
what, if anything, has been learned. If, in observing your lesson, you find
yourself unsure about what effect any activity has had, then see if you can
devise ways of checking on what has been learned from a particular
activity.

Once you are able to teach a lesson with these built-in checks on what is
being learned, you can repeat this task with a different lesson.

Evaluation
How well does your teaching-act analysis of the lesson match with the
learning-effect analysis? Did the students learn what you wanted them to
learn?

Can you pinpoint any activities where there was a mismatch? Can you
account for the mismatch?

► # TASK 145

Aim
To extend Task 144 by getting the students to do their own learning-effect analysis.

Resources
As for Task 144, and a small piece of paper for each student. A recording of the lesson is not necessary.

Procedure
As for Task 144, but at the end of the lesson, present the students with a breakdown of the activities you employed in it, for example:

>   teaching of new words
>   reading aloud of passage

and so on. Ask them to write down opposite each activity what they learned, or what they thought they were supposed to learn from it.

Collect in all the students' responses.

Evaluation
As for Task 144.

12.2 The participants

Tasks 146 to 150 are best done in the order in which they appear here. Task 146 deals with the various combinations of participants in the classroom interaction; Tasks 147 to 149 deal with the experience and expectations of the participants and the effect that these have on classroom teaching and learning; and Task 150 is an optional extra, to use the expertise gained in the previous tasks on another classroom situation.

► # TASK 146

Aim
To see what patterns of interaction operate in your own and your colleagues' classrooms.

Resources
- Several classes, live or recorded, taught by yourselves and your colleagues.
- Diagrams of classroom interaction patterns exemplified in 8.4 above.

Procedure
Observe the classes, and note down the different patterns of pedagogic interaction that occur as the lesson proceeds. Use the categories of

Teacher
Textbook
Whole Class
Groups of Students
Pairs of Students
Individual Students

as participants in the interaction, and show the patterns of interaction in diagram form where possible (on the model of those diagrams in 8.4 above).

Record against each pattern as it occurs the length of time it lasts. Try this exercise over several different classes, in several different types of lesson, and with several different teachers.

Evaluation
What has this exercise revealed to you about your own/other people's teaching?

Can you make any generalizations from your data about the sort of patterns of interaction that predominate in your classes/school?

Can you see any correlation between types of interaction pattern and type of lesson/teacher, and so on?

▶ **TASK 147**
Aim
To draw up a learner profile/learner profiles for your class.

Resources
– The class you take most frequently/know best.
– The list of features of experience and expectations mentioned in 8.4 above.

Procedure
Use the list of features involved in learner experience and expectations that were mentioned in 8.4 to build up a learner profile for your own class. Ensure that the profile gives a detailed description of the learners in terms of their

general knowledge/knowledge of the world
educational experience and expectations
linguistic experience and expectations.

It may be that your class is a fairly homogeneous group, in which all the students come from roughly the same type of background and have shared the same type of experience. It may be that your students are more of a mixed group, with widely differing backgrounds, in which case you will have to draw up several different learner profiles accordingly. You will probably need to talk to students, both individually and as a group, at some length in order to build up comprehensive learner profiles.

Evaluation

Have you discovered anything new about your students as a result of this exercise? If so, what have you discovered?

Have you been surprised by any of the discoveries you have made about them?

► TASK 148

Aim

To see how well the learner profile(s) drawn up in Task 147 match the profile of yourself as teacher.

Resources
– The list of features mentioned in 8.4 above.
– The profile(s) drawn up in Task 147 above.

Procedure

First draw up a teacher profile for yourself on exactly the same lines as the learner profile(s) you drew up in the preceding task. Add any other information to the profile that you feel is relevant.

Then compare this teacher profile with the learner profile(s) for your class, looking for any points of difference between them.

Evaluation

How well do teacher and learner profiles match? Are there any important areas of mismatch?

Do you think that any mismatch, if it exists, can affect your teaching of that particular class in any way? If so, in what ways? How could the mismatch, and any influence on teaching and learning resulting from it, be resolved?

► TASK 149

Aim

To see how well the profiles of different learners within the class group match.

Resources

Learner profiles drawn up in Task 147 from a mixed group class.

Procedure

If you had to draw up various different learner profiles for Task 147, try comparing them now. Look for significant areas of mismatch between the different learner profiles you drew up.

Evaluation

How well do the different learner profiles match? Are there any instances of serious mismatch? In what areas? If there is any mismatch, could this affect the teaching and learning that goes on in the class? In what way(s)? How could you adapt your teaching to take account of the sorts of differences between learners that you have identified here?

 ## TASK 150

Aim

To draw up, and match, teacher and learner profiles for another class that you are not acquainted with.

Resources

A teacher and class significantly different from your own class that provided you with the data for Tasks 147 to 149 above.

Procedure

Set about drawing up a learner profile/learner profiles for the class in the same way as you did for your own class in Task 147. Gather the necessary information through class discussion, individual interviews, and/or questionnaires.

Then draw up a teacher profile for the class's teacher in the same way as you drew one up for yourself in Task 148. Unless this is a colleague you know well, you will have to interview him or her thoroughly to get the information you need.

If the class is a very mixed group, do a repeat of Task 149 with the learner profiles. Then match the teacher and learner profiles in the same way as you did for your own class in Task 148. Look out for any instances of serious mismatch between the profiles.

Evaluation

On the basis of drawing up and matching profiles like this, what advice would you offer the teacher on how best to handle his or her class? What warnings would you give about possible areas of difficulty in his or her treatment of the class?

12.3 Setting

Tasks 151 to 153 should be attempted in the order in which they appear here, since each task adds something to the previous one until a comprehensive picture of setting can be built up in the final task. Task 154 can be done either here, at the beginning of the series of tasks on setting, or where it is, at the end, since it explores your own attitudes to the setting in which you teach.

► TASK 151

Aim
To see how your immediate classroom setting influences the way you teach.

Resources
— Your classroom/the classroom in which you do most of your teaching.
— Your subject syllabus and school curriculum.

Procedure
Think of the next language lesson you are due to teach. List features of the immediate classroom setting for that lesson under headings of:

       physical features
       temporal features
       psycho-social features
       educational features

as outlined in 8.5 above.

Evaluation
What effect, if any, do the features on your list have on the methodological activities and techniques employed in the lesson you are about to teach? If none, should they have an effect?

► TASK 152

Aim
To see how features of the school or educational institution in which you work influence your teaching.

Resources
A thorough knowledge of your school/educational institution.

Procedure
Exactly as in Task 151 above, but this time you are listing under the four headings features of your school/educational institution, and not just features of the classroom in which you teach.

Evaluation
What effect, if any, do the features on your list have on your teaching? If none, should they have an effect?

► TASK 153

Aim
To see how features of the country/region in which you teach influence your teaching.

Resources
A thorough knowledge of the country/region in which you are teaching, and of its culture.

Procedure
Exactly the same as in Tasks 151 and 152 above, but this time you should list under the four headings relevant features of the country or region in which you teach.

Evaluation
What effect, if any, do the features on your list have on your teaching? If none, should they have some effect?

 TASK 154

Aim
To get a complete picture of the setting in which you teach.

Resources
Your lists from Tasks 151 to 153 above.

Procedure
Fill in the grid (Table 9) on the basis of information from the lists you drew up in Tasks 151 to 153 above.

	Physical	Temporal	Psycho-social	Educational
Country				
School				
Classroom				

Table 9

Evaluation

Can you see any links between different sections of the grid? If so, what are they?

Do the various levels match? If there is any mismatch between levels under the same headings, can you account for it?

Is your classroom typical of the institution/country in which it is located? Is your school/teaching institution typical of the country/region in which it is located?

► ## TASK 155

Aim

To examine your own attitudes to setting.

Resources

– A quiet half-hour for reflection, or small-group discussion.
– Your work on Tasks 152 to 154 above.

Procedure

Ask yourself how you view the features of setting listed in the grid in Task 154, as either

a. constraints on your teaching, in that they prevent you from teaching as you would like to teach; or
b. guides to help you plan your teaching in the most effective manner.

If your response is (a), state how you would like to teach if there were no constraints. Consider how you might ease current constraints to enable you to teach as you would like. If your response is (b), give examples of ways in which the features of your own setting have helped to guide your teaching.

Evaluation

If your answer was (a), were you surprised that features of setting could be seen as (b), and vice versa?

Glossary

acceptable: the second condition for an utterance to be communicatively effective, in that it does not cause offence or create conflict between participants in the communicative event.

accessible: the first condition for an utterance to be communicatively effective, in that it should be clear what the speaker's intentions are in making the utterance.

activity: what the teacher does, or makes the students do, in the classroom in order to present or practise the target language.

addressee: the person to whom an utterance is directed.

addresser: the person who makes the utterance.

affect: feelings, emotion.

authentic: when applied to text this means 'not specially written for pedagogic purposes'.

classroom observation: watching what goes on in the classroom for various purposes e.g. research, teacher-training, maintenance of teaching standards, and so on.

code: a system used for communication purposes in order to transmit a message between people.

communication: the successful transmission of a message between people.

communication game: a classroom activity involving communication in the target language, but with some non-linguistic aim in view, e.g. the drawing of a picture, construction of a model, arrangement of a series of pictures, and so on.

communicative purpose: the aim or intention behind communication, the reason for communicating.

content: in 'propositional content', the topic of, or matter treated in, an utterance.

context: the setting in which a communicative event takes place.

Counselling Language Learning: an approach to language teaching based on principles of psychological counselling.

curriculum: course of study, embracing all subjects, at an educational institution, or within a national education system.

discourse: language being put to use in communicative events.

discourse analysis: attempts to describe discourse.

false beginners: learners who seem to have zero command of the target language but who have studied it at some point in their previous careers.

form: as opposed to meaning, refers to the abstract characterization of language, the characteristics of a piece of language in terms of the structure of the language system.

function: the use to which a piece of language is put in a social context to communicate messages of different types.

functional approach: an approach to language teaching which views the functional use of language (as opposed to its syntactic form, semantic content, etc.) as of primary importance.

'Humanistic' approaches/techniques: approaches to/activities in language teaching which emphasize affective factors and interpersonal aspects of the classroom situation.

illocutionary force: in speech act theory, refers to the act which a speaker performs in making an utterance.

interactant: one of the participants involved in interaction.

interaction: a process in which people/things have a reciprocal effect upon each other through their actions: as opposed to transaction, the interpersonal aspects of the communicative event.

interaction analysis: the attempt to describe the interaction process.

learning effect: the effect of any teaching act upon the learner(s) to whom it is directed.

live: as opposed to recorded, refers to samples of classroom interaction as it actually occurs in the classroom.

medium: the means whereby a message is transmitted, with reference to speech, writing, and so on.

message: the substance of communication, the matter to be transmitted from sender to receiver.

methodology: the system used for the communication of teaching points from teacher to learner(s).

mnemonics: devices for helping the memory, e.g. (for English spelling) '"i" before "e" except after "c"'.

observation instruments: tools designed for description of classroom interaction (different aspects of this according to the purpose for which the description is being done) by an observer watching the lesson without participating in it.

participant: one of those taking part in a communicative event.

pedagogy: the science/art of teaching.

perlocutionary effect: in speech act theory, refers to the act performed when an utterance has a particular effect on the person to whom it is directed.

précis: abstract of a text; the message of a text expressed in a condensed economic form.

propositional content: the subject matter of an utterance.

purpose: aim, goal, intention.

reaction: an act in response to a previous action/a state which arises as a result of a particular action.

remedial class: a class of learners who have previously studied/made some progress in the target language, but need to have many basic errors in, and misconceptions about, the language sorted out.

rod: a cuisenaire rod, used in the 'Silent Way'; essentially a small, long and thin block of wood in a primary colour.

setting: the context, in both physical and temporal terms, in which a communicative event takes place.

Silent Way: an approach to language teaching which minimizes the speaking role of the teacher.

skills: in language-teaching terms, this refers to the four basic language skills of listening, speaking, reading, and writing.

speech act: a view of the utterance in relation to the behaviour of the speaker and the hearer involved in the communicative event.

speech event: the basic unit used in the analysis of verbal interaction; the manifestation of a communicative event using language as a code.

structure: the manner of organization of elements within a system.

substitution drill: an exercise in which learners have to replace one item with another at a particular point in a structure (normally a sentence).

Suggestopedia: an approach to learning, particularly language learning, based on psychological principles of the power of suggestion.

syllabus: a programmed course of studies for a specific subject in the curriculum.

teacher-controlling: refers to teaching materials which do not allow the teacher much freedom of choice in how he or she uses them.

teaching force: the intention behind the choice of activity employed by the teacher.

total physical response: an approach to language teaching where activities require the learners to engage in some form of physical action.

transformation drill: an exercise in which learners are required to transform one structure into another, such as a positive into a negative, a simple present statement into a simple past statement.

word-attack skills: skills which enable a reader/listener to work out the meaning of words that he or she is unfamiliar with, e.g. guessing meaning from context, deriving the meaning of a word from knowledge of suffixes and/or prefixes, and so on.

Further reading

The books and papers listed in the References will provide further elaboration of the issues dealt with in Sections One and Two. The following is a brief selection of other books which have a general bearing on these issues. The references they in turn provide will give guidance for readers who wish to undertake more extensive exploration.

A **On language and communication**

R. M. Coulthard: *An Introduction to Discourse Analysis* (new edition). London: Longman, 1985.

The best initiation into the field in general: it combines authority with clarity of presentation.

J. C. Richards and **R. W. Schmidt** (eds.): *Language and Communication.* London: Longman, 1983.

A collection of papers which provide a straightforward introduction to different topics in the field.

B **On the description of classroom interaction**
S. Delamont: *Interaction in the Classroom.* London: Methuen, 1976.

M. W. Stubbs and **S. Delamont:** *Explorations in Classroom Observation.* New York: John Wiley, 1976.

These books both deal with classroom interaction in general. With regard to interaction in the language classroom, the following collection of papers is informative (if not easy) reading:

H. W. Seliger and **M. H. Long** (eds.): *Classroom Oriented Research in Second Language Acquisition.* Rowley, Mass.: Newbury House, 1983.

C **Classroom methodology**
E. W. Stevick: *Memory, Meaning and Method.* Rowley, Mass.: Newbury House, 1976.

E. W. Stevick: *Learning Languages: A Way and Ways.* Rowley, Mass.: Newbury House, 1980.

These books are probably the best introductions to language-teaching approaches which particularly focus on teacher/learner interaction. For a more particular and personal perspective on action and interaction in the language classroom, see

C. J. Brumfit: *Communicative Methodology in Language Teaching.* Cambridge: Cambridge University Press, 1984.

Bibliography

Austin, J. L. 1962. *How to Do Things with Words.* Oxford: Clarendon Press.

Bowers, R. 1980. 'Verbal Behaviour in the Language Teaching Classroom.' PhD thesis, University of Reading.

British Council. 1979. *Communication Games.* London: English Language Teaching Institute.

British Council. 1982. *Humanistic Approaches: an Empirical View (ELT Documents 113).* Oxford: Pergamon Press.

British Council. 1985. *Teaching and Learning in Focus* (video tapes with support material). London: The British Council.

Brown, G. 1975. *Microteaching.* London: Methuen.

Byrne, D. 1965. *Elements of Direct and Indirect Speech* (in *Elements of English* series). London: Longman.

Curran, C. 1972. *Counseling-Learning: A Whole-Person Approach for Education.* Illinois: Apple River Press.

Flanders, N. A. 1970. *Analysing Teaching Behavior.* Reading, Mass.: Addison-Wesley.

Gattegno, C. 1972. *Teaching Foreign Languages in Schools: The Silent Way.* New York: Educational Solutions Inc.

Hymes, D. H. 1962. 'The ethnography of speaking' in T. C. Gladwin and W. D. Sturtevant (eds.): *Anthropology and Human Behavior.* Washington, DC: Anthropological Society of Washington.

Lozanov, G. 1978. 'The suggestopedic method of teaching foreign languages' in *Second Language Acquisition and Maintenance.* Washington, DC: ATESOL.

Mitchell, R. and **B. Parkinson.** 1979. 'A Systematic Linguistic Analysis of the Strategies of Foreign Language Teaching in the Secondary School.' BAAL conference paper: mimeo.

Moore, J. (ed.) 1979. *Reading and Thinking in English.* The British Council and Oxford University Press.

Moskowitz, G. 1976. 'The classroom interaction of outstanding language teachers.' *Foreign Language Annals* 9/2.

Moskowitz, G. 1978. *Caring and Sharing in the Foreign Language Class.* Rowley, Mass.: Newbury House.

Royal Society of Arts Examinations Board. 1984. Check List and Report on Practical Test for Diploma for Overseas Teachers of English. London: RSA.

Rubin, J. and **L. Thompson.** 1982. *How to Be a More Successful Language Learner*. Boston, Mass.: Heinle and Heinle.

Searle, J. R. 1969. *Speech Acts: An Essay in the Philosophy of Language*. Cambridge: Cambridge University Press.

Sinclair, J. McH. and **R. M. Coulthard.** 1975. *Towards an Analysis of Discourse*. Oxford: Oxford University Press.

Stern, H. H. 1983. *Fundamental Concepts in Language Teaching*. Oxford: Oxford University Press.

Ullman, R. and **R. Geva.** 1984. 'Approaches to observation in second language classes' in C. J. Brumfit (ed.): *Language Issues and Education Policies (ELT Documents 119)*. Oxford: Pergamon Press.

Widdowson, H. G. 1984. *Explorations in Applied Linguistics 2*. Oxford: Oxford University Press.

Willis, J. 1981. *Teaching English Through English*. London: Longman.